IT and the East

Other Gartner, Inc. Books from Harvard Business School Press

*Heads Up: How to Anticipate Business Surprises
and Seize Opportunities First*
by Kenneth G. McGee

*The New CIO Leader: Setting the Agenda and
Delivering Results*
by Marianne Broadbent and Ellen S. Kitzis

*Multisourcing: Moving Beyond Outsourcing to
Achieve Growth and Agility*
by Linda Cohen and Allie Young

IT and the East

HOW CHINA AND INDIA ARE ALTERING THE FUTURE OF TECHNOLOGY AND INNOVATION

James M. Popkin

Partha Iyengar

Gartner, Inc.

HARVARD BUSINESS SCHOOL PRESS

Boston, Massachusetts

No part of this publication may be reproduced, stored in or introduced into a retrieval system, or transmitted, in any form, or by any means (electronic, mechanical, photo-copying, recording, or otherwise), without the prior permission of the publisher. Requests for permission should be directed to permissions@hbsp.harvard.edu, or mailed to Permissions, Harvard Business School Publishing, 60 Harvard Way, Boston, Massachusetts 02163.

Library of Congress Cataloging-in-Publication Data

Popkin, James M.
  IT and the East : how China and India are altering the future of
technology and innovation / James M. Popkin, Partha Iyengar.
     p. cm.
  ISBN-13: 978-1-4221-0314-2 (hardcover : alk. paper)
  1. High technology industries—Technological innovations—China. 2.
High technology industries—Technological innovations—India. 3.
Technological innovations—Economic aspects—China. 4. Technological
innovations—Economic aspects—India 5. China—Foreign economic
relations—India. 6. India—Foreign economic relations—China. I.
Iyengar, Partha. II. Title.
  HC430.H53P52 2006
  338'.0640951—dc22

                                                        2006034705

The paper used in this publication meets the minimum requirements of the American National Standard for Information Sciences—Permanence of Paper for Printed Library Materials, ANSI Z39.48-1992.

Contents

Part Two. India

Part Three. Chindia

Acknowledgments

Writing a book requires the work and contributions of many people. It was our great fortune to have been able to collaborate with one of the true thought leaders of our time and a former colleague at Gartner, Bob Hayward. Bob's vision and ability to articulate are only matched by his encyclopedic knowledge of all things having to do with information and communications technology in Asia Pacific.

Inspiration has come from colleagues, guides, teachers, and peers, who gave us unqualified support for this research and analysis. We note especially the contributions of Sujay Chohan, Dion Wiggins, Hong Gang and his AMA Infotech Team, and all of the Gartner analysts in China and India. Melissa Martin and Sandra Lahtinen of the Gartner Library Resource Center were invaluable for their unending supply of information, reference material, and good humor.

Gartner management has been especially supportive of this effort. We thank Peter Sondergaard, Senior Vice President of Gartner Research, for allowing us to pursue our passion around this book. We thank Andrew Spender at Gartner Press for his guidance and financial support. Heather Levy of Gartner Press deserves special recognition for her leadership and encouragement. She spurred us on even through childbirth (hers, not ours)—Heather, your commitment to this book was unparalleled.

As with every book of this nature, its very existence is owed to the writing and editing talents of a persistent and faithful group: Tim Ogden, who dragged us into this in the first place; Stuart Washington, who is the fastest writer in the east, north, west, and south; and Ann-Maree Moodie for her valued contributions.

Two others from this talented team deserve special recognition. Jacque Murphy, our gracious and patient editor from Harvard Business School Press who never lost faith in us, thank you. Tom Hayes has an uncanny ability to listen, write, tape-record, and synthesize volumes of data and Gartner analyst ramblings that would have humbled a lesser man. Thank you, Tom, for all of the late nights and early mornings. One day we may even be able to publish the underground "San Francisco Sessions."

The methodologies, frameworks, and analytical reasoning for this book come from the Gartner research culture. The strength and foundation of the methodologies and frameworks are a credit to Gartner. Any flaws in reasoning and logic belong to the authors.

We would also like to add a note of thanks to Gartner clients, many of whom, especially in China and India, have provided key inputs and comments during the writing of this book and in serving as informal peer reviewers. The formal peer reviewers, who provided valuable feedback and insights, have also made this a much better book than it otherwise would have been.

Jamie's involvement in this book was only made possible by the love and support of his family. Greta, Maddy, and Sam—thank you for coming on a great adventure with me.

Partha thanks his wife Jhumkee for her constant support and encouragement, as well as for being an excellent sounding board for ideas, and his children, Rishi and Mitul, for their cheerful involvement and understanding during the writing of this book.

Partha dedicates this book to the memory of his father.

IT and the East

As INDUSTRY ANALYSTS, we continually seek to uncover major, far-reaching trends that will affect both our clients and the IT industry. We look for the inexorable patterns, seminal events, and startling decisions whose global reach defines eras.

The hottest topic in the high-tech industry today is the prominence of China and India.[1] If you are a strategist or a decision maker in almost any enterprise, anywhere in the world, you see the impact of India and China in new waves of technology products and services, events, decisions, and strategies featured on corporate Web sites, and in international news coverage.

As analysts, we have been fortunate to travel extensively in China, India, and virtually everywhere else in the world where the impact of these two rising economic giants is felt. Wherever we have gone over the last three years, we have been consumed with answering our clients' questions about China and India. These experiences inspired us to speculate about what lies ahead for each country and to seriously consider the idea of "Chindia"—a combined China and India competing globally in several industries—as a subject for research and analysis. The Chindia framework is offered as a means to explain how these two great countries might soon reassert their combined influence on the international stage.

The growing impact of China and India in the IT industry is clear to anyone following the money of global trade. It would be hard to match nine days in the spring of 2006 for emphatic statements from chief executives of global corporate giants about the future appeal of these fast-growing economies.

General Electric's Jeffrey Immelt, marking the one hundredth anniversary of GE's first step into China, said in Beijing that GE's $5 billion revenues in China "could double" in the next four or five years.[2] "I think we're still in the early days of being able to grow this market," he added.[3] The next day, in India's Mumbai financial district, Immelt told a business audience that GE had sharply increased revenue targets in India to $8 billion by 2010.[4] "India is a market set to realize its potential," he said. "The next 10 years are critically important" for its infrastructure and economic growth.[5]

A week later, IBM's Samuel Palmisano stood in Bangalore before more than ten thousand company employees and guests, including India's president A. P. J. Abdul Kalam, and announced with flair that IBM would triple its investment in India to $6 billion through 2009. "If you are not here in India, making the right investments and finding and developing the best employees and business partners," he said, "then you won't be able to combine the skills and expertise here with skills and expertise from around the world in ways that can help . . . clients be successful. I'm here today to say IBM is not going to miss this opportunity."[6]

We have not missed the opportunity to share our thoughts and insights with you. This book is written specifically to help CIOs and other IT decision makers of global enterprises and leaders and strategists of companies in the global IT industry to examine in a disciplined way how best to pursue their future in China and India. Whether customers or creators of IT products and services, these enterprises are building a global IT industry in which the economies and talents of China and India loom ever large.

We do not specifically address the priorities and perspectives of executives leading businesses based in China or in India—many of whom are our clients and friends—yet we are confident that they will find valuable insights here as well. We believe this will also be the case for government officials and investors around the world. We know from our research and consulting activity that they are deeply interested in the themes of this book.

IT Innovation Moves Westward

The center of the technology world has been moving steadily west for two hundred years. The innovation that drove the industrial revolution was based in England. For decades the British crown maintained strict export controls on technology and people to prevent the movement of physical and intellectual capital out of the United Kingdom. As always, however, restrictions failed, and eventually the knowledge and experts escaped, moving the center of innovation to the United States, with its large local market and freedom to pursue new opportunities.

With strong investment in education, a high degree of economic freedom, and strong intellectual property protection, the United States remained the world capital of innovation and technology. The next great wave of technology advances began just a few miles away from where the first industrialized factories in the United States were built. The computer age began in and around Boston, Massachusetts, specifically, along the corridor defined by Route 128, where Digital Equipment, Data General, Lotus Development, and dozens of other world-class innovators thrived. As the personal computer overtook large machines, the center of innovation moved west again, primarily to Silicon Valley in California. Here, Intel, Hewlett-Packard, and Oracle grew to rule the day.

Another westward shift has been underway since the mid-1990s. But the new center will not be in the Western world at all. Today China and India are producing some of the world's best-trained computer science and electrical engineering graduates. Far from being simply a source of cheap labor, both countries soon will be able to compete favorably for global business—as India's IT services firms have done—not on price, but on competence and capability. Even more crucial to their increasing global predominance is the rapid growth of domestic markets for technology and consumers in China and India. Soon both countries will have spending power equal to the United States and Western Europe.

Much of the West's mainstream attention on China and India thus far has focused on the West's outsourcing of manufacturing and low-end service jobs. Optimistic observers believe the current flow of jobs across the Pacific is immaterial in the long run because innovation remains strong in Western countries, and innovation produces new jobs and economic growth. This view is absolutely correct on the surface, but it hides the underlying truth of what is happening in India and China today: both countries are getting better at driving technological innovation. More and more, traditional Western high-tech firms are sourcing not just the assembly of their products from India and China but also the innovation that drives these products.

These are game-changing developments for global players in the IT industry. Many enterprises are deciding to act today, and the choices they make vary widely. IBM has sold its PC business to the Chinese company Lenovo and declared a major expansion in India. Every major IT outsourcing firm (including Accenture, CSC, EDS, and IBM) and most major IT software companies (CA, IBM, Oracle, SAP) and hardware vendors (IBM, Intel, Motorola, Sun, Texas Instruments) have opened operations in India.

Apple Computer uses outsourced manufacturing in China, sources much of its technology innovation from India, but it is careful to note on all of its products that they are "Designed by Apple in California." Apple also investigated, but rejected, establishing a technical support center in Bangalore.[7] Microsoft, Google, and Yahoo! have "voluntarily" censored their Chinese Internet portals, disallowing such words and phrases as *freedom*, *democracy*, *demonstration*, and *human rights* to comply with Chinese government policy—steps that subsequently incurred the wrath of the U.S. Congress.[8] Meanwhile, both Google and Yahoo! have taken major stakes in Chinese search and e-commerce companies. Dell—no stranger to putting its brand on products designed and manufactured far from its headquarters in Round Rock, Texas—increasingly turns to Indian and Chinese companies for innovative products.

If you are in a business, you need a China strategy and you need an India strategy. You need to monitor how China and India create alliances in specific markets, alliances under what is coming to be known as the "Chindia bloc." The first signs are already clear in IT services, in automotive components, and in a few other sectors.

China and India increasingly will be the dominant economic stories on the world stage, a trend that may well extend through most of the twenty-first century. Despite mounting stakes, however, the quality of information, research, and advice on how to make key decisions related to China and India is uneven. Executives and managers need a comprehensive view not only for understanding China and India, separately as well as together, but also for gauging future threats to and opportunities for enterprise.

For effective decision making, business leaders need

- accurate information on the current state of global IT competitiveness in India and China and their internal markets;

- a set of realistic scenarios that explores not only the possibility of continued rapid economic growth in India and China but also potential social, political, or other disruptions to these economies;

- a series of milestones that define pivotal issues in each scenario and of signposts that over time point to milestone outcomes to help determine when and where to invest, cooperate, compete, analyze, or ignore these countries.

As the world's largest research and advisory firm in the IT industry, with more than one thousand analysts and consultants, Gartner, Inc. understands the vital role of the IT technology industry in generating and sustaining national economies, and we frequently apply multidimensional research analysis on clients' behalf. In addition, we generate thousands of reports each year rooted in this strategy. Gartner has more than a hundred analysts in India, China, and neighboring countries who cover dozens of vertical IT markets and broader IT industry trends. This global research network is in regular contact with business leaders and government officials in the West and the East and has been a rich and reliable source for much of the information and analysis in this book.

The book is organized to deliver on the above three requirements for effective decision making. The first section focuses exclusively on China; the second, exclusively on India. The third section examines the significant possibilities of China and India combining their complementary economic strengths to compete for world dominance in many industries, including IT.

In our work at Gartner, we use our own methodology and analytical frameworks in combination with a scenario generation framework developed by the consulting firm GBN and featured in Peter Schwartz's book *The Art of the Long View*.[9] The purpose of building these scenarios is to help our clients plan for an uncertain future. These scenarios are not simple predictions; rather, they recognize that some significant market dynamics in each country are genuinely uncertain.

The scenarios for each country identify these critical uncertainties and define several alternative futures. They provide the ability for readers to create useful strategic plans that effectively take into account current reality, future possibility, and risk. The critical uncertainties are presented as a range of possibilities on a continuum, depicted on the two axes of a two-dimensional chart.

For each country we present three scenarios for future developments that are based on the likely outcomes of critical yet uncertain country-specific market dynamics. The three scenarios present the implications for the high-tech industry and are ranked according to our current assessment of the most likely outcomes. Gartner uses a non-mathematical probability metric to compare scenarios and to express our relative confidence in each. This three-scenario approach, we believe, is critical, considering the huge numbers of variables that may affect these countries in the coming years. Leaders must make plans according to the most likely scenarios, but they must also, given the uncertainties, have realistic contingency plans in place.

Our scenario analysis for China is presented in chapter 3; our analysis for India is in chapter 6. A third analysis, projecting various Chindia scenarios, is presented in chapter 8. In these chapters, we identify key milestones that we believe will shape the alternative scenarios, respectively, for China, India, and Chindia during the next several years. For each milestone we identify signposts that indicate whether the most likely outcomes might be changing, and, if so, which of the less likely scenarios appears to be on the rise.

For example, we see the Beijing Olympics, federal budget priorities set in Beijing and New Delhi, and outcomes of the Indian national elections in 2009 as major milestones shaping how the Chindia story unfolds. We conclude that in another ten years a strategic exchange of complementary skills and resources could begin to create unassailable positions for China-India alliances in many global markets. These include several sectors in manufacturing, IT services, textiles, pharmaceuticals, and other industries.

Chapter 9 presents eight high-priority steps to take now to prepare your enterprise for the most likely scenarios. We also specify action steps and competencies you can develop to take advantage of the many opportunities for building IT business in these countries. Organizations that are willing to invest in expert local resources to navigate government policy formulation and rural development programs can influence these areas for their own interests. Recruitment managers should understand how to hire and train local talent, especially in management, and how to weave them into their workforce. And Westerners pursuing IT business in the East must embrace important cultural distinctions that can make or break relationships.

If you have not had to do so already, you will very soon be required to choose how to engage with China and India. As GE's Immelt says, "The new competitors, China and India, are unlike any competitors we have seen in our lifetime."[10] The first chapter begins our story of how the unprecedented dynamics of these new competitors—separate and together—have come to be and where they might be heading.

PART ONE

China

China

REALITY VERSUS PERCEPTION

JUST PAST the Lo Wu border crossing into the People's Republic of China are signs of the great power China is becoming in world affairs. First, there are the stores with counterfeit CDs and DVDs and their attached roving salesmen. Leaving aside the illegalities, here is raw, unvarnished commerce happening before your eyes. Walk a little further to see the whole shining edifice of Shenzhen, with its skyscrapers, Hong Kong–style bustle, and streets crowded with cars.

To the Western visitor, this hubbub of mercantilism and modernity indicates that China has "made it." The crowded streets suggest that China, having released itself from the most burdensome aspects of its Communist past, its poverty, and its peasant masses, is now walking freely toward a bright future.

A little over twenty-five years ago this city simply did not exist. An edict of recently installed Communist Party leader Deng Xiaoping made the rice fields next to the village of Shenzhen China's first special economic zone in August 1980.[1] Shenzhen's explosive growth since then is a potent illustration of China's expanding economic might. Shenzhen, a thriving city of twelve million people and a preeminent industrial base of China, was created by a government directive within a generation.

A recurring theme of this book is that the power China can wield will affect every major corporation in the world. Every business, whether directly engaged with China's economy or not, must have a China strategy. Simultaneously, China will be transforming the information technology industry in ways that executives and managers in the West simply must address. This is true for companies that embrace advancing IT for strategic and operational advantages and especially for hardware and software companies competing anywhere in the full range of IT product and service sectors. When one considers China and India together—as the third section of this book does—the scale of these countries' potential long-term impact on IT competition becomes even greater.

But the future is by no means certain. As shown in forthcoming chapters, China's ability to achieve its vast potential is threatened by both ubiquitous central government participation in the economy and the country's tepid performance to date in creating world-class innovation—perhaps the key driver for a nation's long-term gains in productivity and standards of living.

Continuing government control over the most basic levers of the economy is the most significant inhibitor of China's vast potential for innovation. China's ability to set a practical course to ease government influence in its economy and to promote innovation is *the* pivotal issue in forecasting the country's future. Your first reaction to this might be that government policies and government relations are not my specialty and not my problem—lawyers and government relations pros, not CIOs and IT executives, worry about what the politicians and regulators are up to. You place calculated bets on big issues and market trends in cost-effective, innovative IT. With respect to China (and India), such views are flawed and dangerous for business leaders. The Chinese government often is the biggest factor in IT issues and trends, and business leaders can't afford to delegate these relationships or distance themselves from the core analysis. For that reason we explore in detail the government's dominance in market dynamics and its continuing legacy and habits of impeding overall economic innovation in chapter 3. We aim to provide IT strategists and decision makers with the forecasting tools necessary to frame a China strategy that best fits their specific challenges and aspirations, whether they are global purchasers of IT products and services or creators of those products and services.

But an introduction to the historical and social forces of such a vast country must come first. Lying beneath the opportunities, threats, and uncertainties in China's economic future are challenges as basic as water supply, domestic instability, and a rapidly aging population. A misreading of China's history and economy can trip up otherwise savvy Western executives as surely as Shenzhen's towers give an illusion of permanence.

History

In considering China it is useful to remember that China and India accounted for an estimated 75 percent of global gross domestic product about six hundred years ago. Until the fifteenth century, China was a leader in innovations that spread around the world. A relatively benign geography allowed cultural and political unification from 221 BCE, with a relatively homogenous cultural and ethnic background. About 800 million Chinese speak Mandarin and 300 million speak seven other related languages. (Contrast this with the dizzying cultural diversity of India, described in chapter 4.) China's modern borders are home to the first signs of plant and animal domestication (7500 BCE) and the earliest discovered cast iron (around 500 BCE). Subsequent discoveries include paper, the compass, the wheelbarrow, water-driven spinning machines, and gunpowder, making China more innovative and technologically advanced than Europe until the fifteenth century. In 1450 China lost its lead when it abandoned its program of ocean-going treasure fleets because of a dispute at the imperial court.[2]

Notwithstanding the sweep of China's history, its development in recent years has been a unique model of a centralized government largely and successfully implementing market-based reforms. The achievement is considerable, given China's Communist rule since 1949 as a result of a peasant uprising. It is made even more remarkable given seismic social events such as the Great Leap Forward (1959)—a failed attempt to impose a rural socialist model, resulting in a famine that killed thirty million people—and the Cultural Revolution (1966 to 1976)—a systematic purge of Communist, government, and academic ranks, with millions sent to reeducation camps and an estimated twenty million deaths.

China's current strength is perhaps to the credit of a defining Chinese characteristic, namely, a deep-seated pragmatism, with Communist Party leaders seeking solutions from outside the confines of what was a restrictive Communist ideology. In doing so, Chinese leaders have succeeded in gradually liberalizing the national economy while maintaining a strong socialist political center. In contrast, the collapse of the former Soviet Union's political center has not opened a path to the kind of a capitalist economy and increasing democratic freedoms that many in the West had predicted.

In a landmark in China's development toward a market-based economy, party leader Deng Xiaoping traveled to China's south in 1992, visiting the five special economic zones (including Shenzhen) that he had established more than ten years earlier. "Regardless of whether you call it capitalism or socialism, does it raise productivity?" he asked.[3]

A longtime China adviser to global corporations, Lawrence J. Brahm noted this duality in the approach of modern China's leaders in describing Premier Zhu Rongji's reform program in the 1990s: "[He] was simultaneously applying the tools of traditional socialist state intervention alongside those of classic fiscal and monetary policy of a market economy. With no qualms over theoretical conflicts, he managed these apparently opposite mechanisms of economic leverage to guide and, at times, to force China's transitional economy on to the market path."[4]

The reform program pursued by the Communist Party leadership has been momentous and also, importantly for foreign companies, incomplete. It has attempted to address the interlinked problems of state-owned banks making bad loans to poorly performing state-owned enterprises (SOEs). It embarked on a wholesale reform of the banking system and selling or breaking up poorly performing SOEs. In the early 1990s there were an estimated 300 billion renminbi worth of bad loans to SOEs, the equivalent of roughly $40 billion.[5] The bad loans figure in early 2006, it is estimated, had escalated to a still perilous $220 billion, and many studies by Western firms warned of worsening conditions, especially if the Chinese economy cools.[6] At the same time, attempts have been made to reform the central government bureaucracy, addressing corruption among cadres. In March 1998 Zhu announced policies to "reduce the social activities of members." But the culture of gift-giving based on relationships (*guanxi*) is still very much in evidence.

There have been plenty of bruises for foreign companies in this reform process. Investors were startled when the government simply closed the Guangdong International Trust and Investment Corporation in 1998. Until then, foreign investors believed that their loans of $2 billion to the provincial government investment arm had the implicit, if not stated, backing of the Chinese government.

Chinese Characteristics

The current Chinese successes are seen within China as a reemergence, a perspective that in our experience testifies to the national character and seems to indicate a historical long view within Chinese culture. Others view these internal perceptions of China resuming its rightful place in the world as a barely hidden nationalism based on long-held notions of ethnic superiority, with serious ramifications for regional stability. Indeed China's geopolitical ambitions remain a direct threat to Taiwan and Taiwan's closest ally, the United States. In July 2005 China warned that it would resort to nuclear weapons if the United States intervened in a battle between China and Taiwan.[7] But equally important tensions exist with Japan and many other nations.

It is worth noting three peculiarly Chinese characteristics that still predominate in China today, with a significant impact on business dealings. The first, just introduced, is the concept of *guanxi*. Often described to foreigners as the concept of one's trusted network, guanxi has the negative connotation among foreigners of gift-giving leading to corruption. But the concept of guanxi among Chinese goes much further than paying for entertainment at restaurants. The Chinese approach to business is to form a friendship and then, on the basis of that friendship, to complete a transaction. (See "Variations on the Theme of Courting Business Relationships.") This is the opposite of the Western approach of completing a transaction and then, on the basis of that transaction, forming a friendship.

VARIATIONS ON THE THEME OF COURTING BUSINESS RELATIONSHIPS

A large gathering over exotic local cuisine, lubricated with alcohol, extravagant toasts, and lots of singing late into the night is a Western stereotype for courting new business and client relationships in China. In fact there are more—and better—options and intricate variables, as China slowly opens to the global business culture. You will find some more comfortable and more effective than others.

Here is a helpful breakdown of popular "tracks" as recommended by a Western technology executive with long field experience in China—Cyrill Eltschinger, CEO of I.T. UNITED, a China-based tech outsourcing provider:

- **Dinner.** Sharing a meal together plays a central role in Chinese culture. Hosting a large Chinese dinner, with Chinese liquor (*baijiu*) flowing freely, cigars, and maybe a song or two is a classic and always safe bet. "I've learned to sing some Chinese songs, which never fails to delight and amuse my guests," says Eltschinger. Invite interesting friends as well as spouses to come along. Culturally interested people may also appreciate meeting up in a traditional tea house. Note that Karaoke is unsuitable for breaking the ice with high-level contacts. Even worse are hints about the preferred venue being a gentlemen's club.

- **Entertainment and games.** The Chinese love a good game—anything goes, from drinking games to betting on the outcome of your tennis match. The Chinese equally enjoy a classic concert or any other entertaining outing that will give you a chance to get to know each other better. Try to explore mutual interest or shared experiences. Most of all: be sincere in your efforts to get to know each other.

- **Sports.** Golf, tennis, squash, badminton, and horse riding are currently the sports of choice for high-level executives. "If you are good at any of them, this will help you gain both face and friends," says Eltschinger, himself a former badminton champion. Golf appeals to the Chinese sense of building relationships to facilitate business as it provides an ideal platform for easygoing conversation in harmonious surroundings. The sport is gaining in popularity as Chinese culture begins to adapt to global business practices.

- **Business clubs.** Especially if you are staying in China for a longer period of time, this is a great way to quickly build your network. Many of them offer a combination of meeting rooms and top-notch catering in luxurious surroundings—just the right setting to mix business and pleasure.

- **Feng shui.** This ancient practice for seeking harmony with the environment has its origins in Taoism and is deeply embedded in Chinese culture. Most Chinese will be aware of these teachings at some level. Throughout China, fish are a symbol of good fortune and prosperity. Feng shui can also help you find an auspicious location for closing your business deal. Employ the services of an expert, if you want to go for it.

- **Gifts.** Traditionally, gifts are exchanged to express mutual goodwill and appreciation. If you know someone's interest, a small personal gift will help you build your friendship. Be aware that depending on the size and nature of the gift, this track may violate Western corporate ethical standards.

- **Overseas trip.** Subsidize an overseas trip for a conference or trade show, holiday, or shopping trip. While this is common in Asia, be aware that this may violate Western corporate ethical standards.

Source: Cyrill Eltschinger, interview notes via e-mail to Jamie Popkin, September 6, 2006.

The second characteristic is for Chinese to consider business negotiations in a very holistic sense, in contrast to a very linear, targeted approach taken in Western business. This can be downright confusing for Western companies, which are forced to respond to what seem (to them) to be queries remarkably unrelated to the transactions presumed to be at hand.

The third characteristic that should be borne in mind is a deep, ingrained culture in China of accepting authority and the associated concept of "face," the importance of retaining the respect of others. Singaporean academic Ng Aik Kwang points to the roots of face in social differences with Western countries, including the tightly organized nature of Asian societies, the greater emphasis in Asia on the group rather than the individual, and a greater emphasis in Asia on social order and harmony.[8]

Economics

The economics of China today are convoluted and much more sobering than the storefront gloss offered by the super cities of Shanghai and Beijing would suggest. The per capita gross national income of China is $1,290 annually, compared with $41,400 in the United States.[9] Despite all the worries in the West about China's economic ascendancy, the average annual income in the United States is more than thirty times greater than average per capita income in China. Yet even this figure misrepresents the actual situation in China, where there are stark differences between the relatively prosperous coastal regions, the old industrial base in the northeast, and the poorest region in the west.

An analysis of per capita gross domestic product by McKinsey & Company, the management consultancy, shows that residents of Shenzhen and Shanghai are earning average figures of more than $6,000 annually; residents of Beijing, about $3,900 annually; and residents of Xining, in China's west, $900 annually.[10] In another deep rift between the wealthy and the poor, China's plentiful rural population survives on even less, with an estimated 44 percent of employment derived from agriculture. There were estimates in 2000 that fifty million Chinese lived below a poverty line of less than sixty cents a day.[11]

Added to this have been the serious social effects and dislocation of the economic reforms. These reforms have been referred to as "breaking the iron rice bowl" of government employment. Despite an official urban unemployment rate of 4.1 percent, the U.S. government puts this figure at 9.8 percent in China's urban areas and cites a Chinese journal's estimate of 20 percent unemployment—or 152 million under- or unemployed.[12]

These great disparities have obvious impacts on business inside China, in terms of location, stability, and internal competitiveness. On the most brutal level, there have been riots of disenfranchised rural workers, with estimates of eighty-seven thousand mass public protests in 2004.[13] And in a corporate move underlining just how competitive China is internally, Unilever moved its manufacturing facility from Shanghai to Anhui Province to achieve a lower-cost base and become more competitive in the local market.[14]

The Communist Chinese Party (CCP) claims that alleviating the great divide in living standards between the wealthier urban coastal regions and the agriculture-dependent rural west is now a major priority. Many programs included in the party's five-year economic plan announced in March 2006 addressed these issues. Global business strategists and IT managers must keep a close eye on whether the payoff in coming years from these central government pledges meets the approval of China's rural poor.

This is by any standard a daunting political challenge. China's rural regions are home to one-eighth of the world's population, or about 800 million people. In these mainly agricultural enclaves, memories of two generations of Maoist anti-intellectual rhetoric and wealth-redistribution programs die hard. Even worse, countless riots and demonstrations in recent years reportedly were incited by episodes of local Communist Party officials seizing farmlands for personal gain without recompensing the peasants who worked the land.

Central party leaders in Beijing know that they must reverse this and other forms of official corruption. They know that they must rapidly spread palpable benefits of market reforms to the countryside—including access to manufacturing jobs, training, and education. While this seems unlikely, failure on these fronts could invite a socialist backlash that would threaten the interests of global companies already active in China with investments, partnerships, and expanding supply-chain dependencies.

Another challenge for business is the confusing, multitiered nature of the current government structure. There are twenty-two provinces, five "autonomous" regions, four municipalities under central government control, and two special administrative regions. In theory, these areas answer to the National People's Congress, a body of three thousand delegates, although the organization is seen as little more than a rubber stamp to approve measures first considered by the twenty-four–member Politburo.

This underlines one of the intricacies of dealing in China—for every level of government there is a corresponding, but slightly more senior, level of the Communist Party, with its own views and ambitions. In dealing with this one-party political environment, foreign companies must bear in mind that one city is not necessarily like the next city. For the visiting foreign national, the intensity of competition and rivalry between regional governments and regional businesses simply defies belief. It flourishes in an environment that allows a high degree of seeming autonomy at the province level. This was evidenced in the 1990s by the "bigger is better" mentality of provincial governments and their unstinting support of edifice building through bad loans to poorly performing state-owned enterprises. Individual provinces also went well beyond centrally mandated norms, with—in just one example—Haikou and Chengdu even establishing their own stock exchanges. In our own experience in talking with seventy IT services providers, Chinese companies display this provincial tendency, actively denigrating and disparaging other cities.

To be sure, the power still held at the center must not be ignored: the central government closed the above-mentioned stock exchanges. In a more recent example, on June 17, 2002, the Chinese government closed an estimated two hundred thousand Internet cafés in one day.[15]

None of this has deterred foreign investors from dramatically increasing their investments in China in recent years. Annual foreign direct investment (FDI) into China rose from $37.5 billion in 1995 to $60.33 billion in 2005, with the U.S. share declining to 5 percent in 2005 from a peak near 11 percent in 2000.[16] China's incredible export success is evidenced by the increase over the same period in its foreign exchange reserves, which have grown from $73.6 billion in 1995 to $819 billion in 2005.[17] In fact, China recorded its first trade surplus with the United States only in the early 1990s; its trade surplus with the United States in 2005 was $201 billion.

China Today

Capitalizing on this investment and export performance, China has successfully proved itself as the factory of the world, using its lower cost of wages to export cheaper goods to willing consumers in predominantly Western countries. The success of this strategy can be seen in its share of global commodities demand: the Asian Development Bank estimates that in 2004 China took 40 percent of the world's steel, 30 percent of its coal, and 25 percent of its aluminum and copper.[18] The internal transformation has been marked by a rise in small, often private enterprises that have contributed greatly to China's performance. Economist Xiao Liang estimated that in 1998 small and medium-sized companies accounted for 60 percent of the nation's industrial production. This trend is reflected in the current state of the information technology market. In a development to be explored in later chapters, there are, by our estimate, currently ten thousand small IT services companies within China. This is far too many, of course. The surfeit of such companies results in part from government officials intervening against market forces to prevent companies from failing.

In a transition with effects yet to be fully recognized, China's reforms have also unleashed the power of Chinese consumers. This is reflected in

World Bank estimates in the change of savings patterns. In 1978, individuals accounted for only 3.4 percent of savings. By 1998, individuals accounted for 83 percent of savings. Telling figures show the power of this consumer market in the IT area. There are now 363 million mobile phone users in China, compared to about 181 million in the United States.[19] In 2000 there were 374 million television sets in China, outnumbering the 243 million television sets in the United States.

China Ongoing

In an optimistic view, China is well placed to build on its successes. Harvard University economist Richard Freeman notes that there were about thirteen thousand science and engineering doctorates awarded in China in 2003, compared with about eighteen thousand science and engineering doctorates awarded annually in the United States. Growth in China and stagnation in the United States, he asserts, means that China is poised to surpass the United States in the awarding of these advanced degrees by 2010. The benefits for China are clear: Freeman points to China's growing attraction as a center for research and development, with the number of research centers growing from fewer than fifty in 1997 to more than six hundred in mid-2004.[20] Many of these centers are funded by global IT companies, including IBM, Intel, and Microsoft.

This trend is fueled by the sheer number of well-educated science and engineering graduates from China. McKinsey estimated that in 2003 China had 8.5 million graduates with up to seven years' professional experience, including 1.6 million engineers. This figure already outstrips the United States, with a total of 7.7 million graduates with up to seven years professional experience, including 700,000 engineers.[21] Freeman reflected powerfully on what could be the natural outcome for the United States and all other developed economies: "By increasing the number of scientists and engineers, highly populous low-income countries such as China and India can compete with the U.S. in technically advanced industries . . . This threatens to undo the traditional 'north-south' pattern of trade in which advanced countries dominate high tech while developing countries specialize in less skilled manufacturing."[22]

But the numbers do not tell the full story. Looking deeper, we find one of the central challenges facing China. The same McKinsey study, based on interviews with eighty-three human resources professionals in multinational companies, found that less than 10 percent of Chinese engineers were suitable for work in a globally competitive enterprise.[23] This perception is shared by China-based companies competing in developed economies.

"Chinese engineers need three-to-six months of company-supplied training to turn them from computer scientists into engineers," said Joseph Hsu, founder and chief executive of the Symbio Group, an IT services firm based in Beijing with more than 90 percent of its clients in the United States. "Scientists are good at free thinking, but engineers need to follow process and work as a team."[24] Symbio's software engineering training program and projects with U.S.-based clients are magnets for recruitment because "Chinese engineers want to work on U.S. projects," he said.[25]

The McKinsey survey also found that the lack of English of a suitable standard was the most pressing issue facing China. McKinsey also raised concerns about standards of higher education within China, noting only 30 percent of 1.7 million graduates in 2003 studied at China's top ten university cities.[26]

Indeed, the most important question facing China today—and its IT industry in particular—is whether the country has the strengths and capabilities to innovate effectively and thus lift itself from being the factory of the world. The challenge is crucial: "No nation will remain the world's low-cost manufacturer forever, and if it were to try to do so, its living standards would stagnate at today's levels."[27]

The second most important, and related, question facing China today is how the government is going to behave when facing the innovation challenge. We have witnessed recent government attempts to promote innovation and control its own destiny. For example, it has launched a series of government-backed technology standards for IT to be used in China in areas as diverse as broadband transmission towers, digital cameras, and high-definition television. On the face of it, this is a strategy designed to reduce reliance on imports, cut prices by eliminating intellectual property (IP) royalties paid to foreign companies, and even to allow China to become a royalty collector if its standards are adopted globally. On a deeper level, however, the Chinese push for standards could simply be a transparent attempt by the government to establish a protectionist framework against foreign companies—with sinister connotations: by setting domestic security standards on wireless communications, the government can decipher encrypted communications. Chapter 3 explores more fully different scenarios regarding China's ability to innovate and the government's willingness to embrace this challenge.

Other challenges that could impede the best possible outcomes for China are legion and threaten to destabilize efforts in every other field. Here are just four examples. China's notoriously conservative state-run media have said that China is facing the world's worst water crisis. China's aging demographic, aided by the one-child policy, soon will burden its nascent economy, with the number of elderly aged sixty-five or above forecast to double to 200 million by 2025. The banking system is staggering under a huge burden of bad loans, estimated at $800 billion or more in 2006 by several Western analysts, and the government is untested in its ability to resolve the problem. Finally, the sheer challenge of bringing infrastructure to a disparate population is illustrated in Gartner research showing that less than 5 percent of the target audience had broadband as of July 2005.[28]

But for businesspeople interested in China's here and now, it is perhaps most relevant to show one example in which China is exerting surprising and unexpected effects on the global business stage.

For some years Gartner has witnessed Chinese technology companies irrationally diversifying their product lines in response to a chronic oversupply of goods. Many Chinese businesses have launched into seemingly unrelated areas offering little advantage, leading to ruinous price competition in almost every category. For example, Kingdee International Software Group has grown rapidly by targeting the domestic packaged application market. Kingdee derives 85 percent of its revenues from product licenses. In June 2004 Kingdee announced the formation of Kingdee Software Technologies (Shanghai) to provide outsourced application management to offshore customers. Yet the company is ill prepared for the challenges of entering this global market, with little outsourcing experience and a lack of skills in pricing, training, and delivery of the projects it is offering.

It is a little-understood fact that the recent spate of Chinese hardware companies buying offshore has been in part spurred by tough domestic operating conditions and the prospect of higher margins in foreign countries. The *Financial Times* reported that this was a motive for Lenovo's purchase in 2005 of IBM's personal computer business.

This ferocity of competition may give seasoned executives pause as they consider opportunities in the Chinese domestic market. It shows that motives of Chinese companies going abroad are not as simple as following the government's directive to *zou chuqu*, literally to "walk outside." Rather, in expanding beyond China's borders, these companies are pursuing their own long-term survival.

But there is no mistaking the power of many Chinese corporations now being built. We have made a set of projections about what the business landscape will look like by 2012. In our view, it is highly probable that at least eight Chinese IT companies will have successfully "gone global" by 2012. And of the top ten international IT and consumer equipment vendors, at least one will be Chinese.

The next chapter considers the springboard for these developments and the current condition of the Chinese information and communications technology market. The final chapter of this first section explores the three most likely scenarios facing China's business and addresses potential responses to these challenges.

two

China's IT Landscape Today

Politicians and interest groups threatened by China's rapid economic ascendance have portrayed the country as a global buccaneer that has overridden intellectual property rights, stolen jobs from developed countries, and wielded its geopolitical muscle. The reality behind the hyperbole is both more mundane and more interesting. It is mundane because China has become the factory of the world. It is interesting because, as China consumes more raw materials from countries near and far to push out goods in astonishing quantities, it is changing the rules for almost every company and country on the globe. China is now the world's largest manufacturer of refrigerators, air conditioners, clocks, televisions, cameras, desktop personal computers, DVD players, and mobile phone handsets.

The blunt challenge for China is to move up the global value chain to the commanding heights of innovation and global marketing prowess. Foreign firms retain an estimated 60 percent of profits generated by China's high-tech exports—a good indication that the Chinese have not yet contributed much creative spark of their own.[1] In IT, the particular challenge for China is to transfer its demonstrated expertise in low-margin, high-volume hardware manufacturing into high-margin software and IT services.

The central government signaled its overall priorities for industrial innovation early in 2006 when it announced its new fifteen-year plan for science and technology. Annual spending by all sources, industry included, is projected to rise to $45 billion, or 2 percent of GDP, in 2010, and to $113 billion, or 2.5 percent of GDP, in 2020. Spending in 2004 was $24.6 billion, or 1.2 percent of GDP. Spending by the central government is set to more than double in 2010, to $18 billion, from $8.7 billion in 2004.[2]

The new priorities lean heavily toward economic development, as opposed to basic research. Protein science, quantum research, nanotechnology, and reproductive biology were among the major science programs. Engineering targets included next-generation mobile phones, large-scale oil and gas exploration, transgenic plant breeding, drug development, and manned exploration of the moon.[3] According to the official Xinhua News Agency, the government also sought "breakthroughs in extreme manufacturing (and) robots capable of doing intelligent services." The agency stated that China's spending on science "is still insufficient, the investment structure is not reasonable and the basic conditions for science and technology are still weak."[4]

Answering the challenge of moving from "made in China" to "made by China" comes down to (1) China's ability to innovate effectively within a restrictive government framework and (2) its human resources potential—a theme that is developed in the scenarios explored in chapter 3. The *current* landscape of the IT industry is not encouraging with respect to China's potential for innovation. The companies within China that are well placed to become global brands are restricted to a handful of hardware manufacturers. These include companies building networking equipment (Huawei, Zhongxing Telecommunications Equipment [ZTE]), mobile handsets (Kejian, Ningbo Bird, Panda Mobile Communications Equipment, and TCL Mobile), computers (Founder Technology Group, Kaifa Technology Group, Lenovo, Langchao Group, Stone Group, and Tongfang), and consumer electronics (Changhong, Galanz

Enterprise Company, Gree Corporation, Haier, Hisense, Kelon, Konka Group, Meiling, Midea, and TCL).[5]

Noteworthy successes in offshore markets notwithstanding, these companies have relied on low-cost strategies and are rarely seen as innovators. Their progress over the past twenty years has not been based on new Chinese technology. According to political scientist Richard P. Suttmeier, China sees itself "unhappily" as a rent payer in the global economy rather than as a rent taker.[6]

If this perspective on Chinese hardware manufacturers is bleak, the outlook is even worse for software and services. There are only a handful of names among an estimated ten thousand software and software services companies that can be advanced comfortably as potential success stories on the global stage. This is despite some software and services companies (for example, Amid, CS&S, Datang Telecom Technology and Industry Group, Genersoft, Kingdee, Neusoft Group, and Ufida) achieving revenues above $100 million domestically in 2004.[7]

Even domestically, as the large number of companies indicates, the industry is highly fragmented and subject to fierce competition. In most cases these software and services companies show little aptitude for becoming serious players globally in IT services provision. This was borne out in Gartner's 2005 examination of seventy Chinese IT outsourcing companies, which revealed a nearly uniform lack of recognition by these companies about the staff capabilities and service levels needed to succeed globally.[8]

Shape and Size

The size and scale of China's domestic IT industry is proportional to its vast population, strong economic growth (10.9 percent in the first half of 2006 and more than 10 percent over the previous three years) leading to strong corporate demand, and excellent record of providing infrastructure. China has the world's largest mobile phone population (estimated at 400 million by December 2006),[9] the world's second largest number of Internet service provider accounts (an estimated 40.6 million in December 2005), and the world's largest number of fixed-access telephone lines (an estimated 312 million in December 2005, up 50 million in one year).[10] As these figures indicate, China is well ahead of India in both per capita and overall numbers. In fact, India's numbers for the same services illustrate starkly the infrastructure challenges it is facing, and the infrastructure benefits China already enjoys. In India in December 2005 there were an estimated 80 million mobile telephone connections, an estimated 7.3 million internet service provider accounts, and an estimated 48 million fixed telephone lines.[11]

China's spending on its IT needs in 2005 was about $119 billion, about four times that of India's. That the majority of this spending went toward telecommunications equipment and services (79 percent) reflects the priorities of an infrastructure that is still growing. China's IT spending has been forecast to grow at 6.5 percent annually through 2009, below the 7.9 percent rate forecast for Asia-Pacific and well below the 25 percent forecast for India.[12] China's IT spending will be led by the purchase of software (17.5 percent) and IT services (14.5 percent). As the software market expands, IT leaders of Western corporations operating in China need to ask, When will locally provisioned software and services be available, and will they be competitive with foreign software and services?

Competition

Foreign IT companies investing in China share a challenge facing domestic IT companies, namely, fierce competition. Though hundreds of articles discuss the barriers to entry, most overlook the fact that China has become one of the most open markets in the world, certainly when measured by the level of foreign investment. (See "The Emerging Culture of Chinese Enterprises in IT.")

THE EMERGING CULTURE OF CHINESE ENTERPRISES IN IT

Multinational corporations have organized wholly foreign-owned enterprises at an accelerating rate since China joined the World Trade Organization in 2001. By shifting R&D centers to China, corporations can take advantage of talented scientists and engineers at low costs to create products and services either directly for Chinese markets or for global markets.

This trend should aid China in transferring technology from the West and improve the country's stature in the global high-tech industry. It also will pressure Chinese colleges and universities to produce more world-class graduates able to compete for positions in global enterprises.

China had 750 foreign-funded R&D centers in early 2006. Many scholars recognize the steady increase in R&D funding by enterprises, as opposed to government, is an important indicator of development for countries trying to create a globally competitive high-tech industry. Chinese enterprises were predominantly government-owned in the 1980s. Now the mix of nongovernment enterprises (NGEs), private, and wholly foreign-owned enterprises (WFOEs) predominates.

Moreover, the Communist Party essentially has accepted Chinese capitalists as members since 2001, when Premier Jiang Zemin announced that private businesspeople could be nominated for membership. NGEs and private enterprises have equal status with state-owned enterprises (SOEs), without undue restrictions to bid for all government projects.

The full range of the information and communications technology (ICT) value chain is being generated by an industry comprised of both domestic and foreign-owned Chinese enterprises. The high-tech industry is a critical part of the nation's overall economic and social development. Major industry achievements resulting from the R&D reforms of the past twenty years include:

- The world's largest telecommunications networks, with more than 370 million mobile subscribers and more than 350 million fixed-line subscribers

continued

- The world's second-largest IP network (after the United States), with more than 110 million users
- The world's largest mobile handset and TV manufacturers
- Lenovo's acquisition of IBM PC to become a global ICT leader
- The rapid rise of Chinese telecom equipment and electronic appliance manufacturers: Huawei, ZTE, UTStarcom, and Haier, all of which have potential to become global brands

Source: Eng Chew, "Education, R&D Institutions Shaping the Chinese ICT Industry," G00138279, Gartner Research, April 13, 2006. Chew holds the Gartner Research Chair of Business and IT Strategy at the Faculty of Information Technology, University of Technology Sydney, New South Wales, Australia. The information and analysis in this box is derived largely from research conducted in collaboration with the Faculty of Information Technology.

On pace in mid-2006 for a third consecutive year of $60 billion or more in foreign direct investment, China is the third most attractive destination for cross-border investing after the United States and England. India, by contrast, has relatively modest foreign direct investment, totaling $5.3 billion in 2004.

For both foreign and Chinese companies, this open economy means a competitive environment at every level: foreign multinational versus foreign multinational, foreign multinational versus domestic company, and domestic company versus domestic company. Illustrating the vigorous competitive landscape for foreign exporters, Ministry of Commerce figures show, for example, that 87 percent of exports of new and high-tech products—a category dominated by IT manufacturers—comes from companies with foreign stakes.

The domestic competitive environment is neatly shown by estimated market shares of domestic IT spending in 2004. Foreign companies dominated spending on telecom equipment (receiving an estimated 65 percent of spending) and IT services (receiving an estimated 90 percent of spending). But domestic companies dominated hardware sales (receiving an estimated 79 percent of spending).[13]

This effect is demonstrated by the successful companies in China in each of the above areas. In telecom equipment, international vendor Nokia is the most successful, followed by Motorola and the Chinese vendor Huawei.[14] In IT outsourcing (a category of IT services) IBM is number one. Gartner has only identified one Chinese company—Lenovo—among the top fourteen vendors.[15] But in hardware sales, Chinese manufacturers Lenovo and Founder hold first and second positions, respectively, in terms of revenue derived from personal computer sales within China to September 30, 2005. Other Chinese companies in the top ten include Tongfang, TCL, and Great Wall. But once again, emphasizing the strong international competition in a very open market, the other major personal computer vendors were the United States' Dell (third) and Hewlett-Packard (fourth), Taiwan's Acer (seventh), and Japan's Toshiba (ninth) and Sony (tenth).[16]

As discussed in the previous chapter, this stark competitive position results in some unexpected and even irrational moves. The competition also creates opportunities in some areas of IT, with outsourcing growing in popularity as cost control comes to the fore. The competition also has the perverse effect of constraining expenditure on research and development at the very time Chinese companies need it most.

In a grim sign for Chinese companies, Nokia clawed its way back into the mobile handset race after previous domination by Chinese vendors by reorganizing its distribution network and localizing its manufacturing. In general, foreign companies operating in China consider their local workforces as diligent and adept at following directions in high-volume, repetitive production tasks. But initiative and originality is widely perceived to be lacking. Indeed, Chinese culture is infused with the Confucian tradition of deference to authority: questioning authority is discouraged at every rite of passage. Classroom learning stresses rote learning and memorization.

For these reasons, creating a capable cadre of middle managers in China-based operations is a major challenge for global companies. "Chinese middle-managers need training in analytical decision making, and knowing their decision rights," notes Jeanne Beyer, an American executive with Objectiva Software Solutions, an IT outsourcing company with operations in Beijing that support clients primarily in the United States. "Information flows in China are very hierarchical. In the U.S. they are flatter and encourage more individual empowerment. Westerners need to understand these differences."[17] Objectiva has turned down offers to partner with Chinese vendors in the China market but expects to find attractive opportunities in China by 2009.

Prospecting for this middle-management talent among the Chinese diaspora—well-trained and highly experienced Chinese based in Western economies—is one solution. So is recruiting onetime Chinese expatriates who have returned to their homeland looking for opportunities to help build the growing economy. These steps are central to staffing strategies that Objectiva and other small, growing IT services firms with primary operations in China are pursuing.

Snapshot of IT Services Firms in China

China's IT services firms are years behind India's in stature and scale. Yet several young firms—typically with headquarters or development operations based in China and sales and client services teams in the United States—have growing relationships with major corporations.

We became very well acquainted with ten firms that were promoting their offerings to hundreds of potential clients at a Gartner conference on IT outsourcing in 2006. All were hand-picked, with all registration and travel expenses covered, by the National Development and Reform Commission (NDRC). These firms often are led by well-credentialed Chinese and Taiwanese expatriates, many of whom were educated in and worked several years for U.S.-based global IT companies.

Joseph Hsu, for example, founder and chief executive of the Symbio Group since 1994, has a master's degree in economics from New York University, worked in IBM's software systems group, and founded an IBM-backed software company in Taiwan in 1987. His Symbio president is a fellow Taiwanese and former IBM colleague, Richard Le. Le is a former head of offshore development projects for IBM's Worldwide Laboratories. "The weakness of many China-based companies is they still think in terms of being a Chinese company," Hsu said. "We have a global DNA. We have Chinese, American, and Indian employees. Our European GM is an Irish citizen, our Japanese team is all Japanese. All the successful India-based outsourcing firms never tell the world they are *Indian* companies."[18]

About 5 percent of Symbio's revenues are generated in China. Hsu is aiming to increase that figure to 20 percent between 2011 and 2016. He expects Japan to surpass the United States as Symbio's largest market. Sales for Symbio in 2006 were $18 million; the company employed seven hundred fifty people.

Objectiva was founded in 1999 by American Douglas Winter and Chinese Tao Ye. They met during graduate studies in business and engineering at the Massachusetts Institute of Technology. Winter, Objectiva's chief executive, is based in California, and Tao, its president, in Beijing.

Hsu and Tao maintain close ties to China's ministries and agencies to promote the IT services industry. Symbio often provides free services to the agencies. "We view the benefits as intangible," Hsu said. "We are well recognized in China, and the government is ready to promote Symbio as a success story."[19]

Tao is a leader in the private sector's Beijing Software Productivity Council and a member of several government committees on IT software. The council's lobbying agenda was crowded in 2006. It included increased financial support for marketing and for standards in credentialing qualified technical specialists, stronger enforcement of intellectual property rights, multilingual signage in Beijing, and better sources of reliable information on the Chinese software industry.[20]

It is quite normal now for China's brightest and best educated to set their own paths in business, not necessarily starting their careers in Chinese enterprises. Many have pursued advanced scientific degrees in developed economies, such as the United States and Australia. Global IT companies have moved quickly to snap up this Chinese talent, offering opportunities to lead research into new processes and applications at their advanced research centers in China. Chinese scholars fear that this "internal brain drain" benefiting global IT organizations will further hinder China's ability to innovate.[21]

State Control

The state remains a formidable presence in any private sector consideration. We have identified seven ministries or offices that are directly responsible for fostering Chinese ambitions in IT. Government policies actively encourage the development of the supply and demand sides of the IT industry.[22] (See "Institutions to Know in China's High-Tech Ecosystem.")

But state control goes much further than this within China. Despite the appearance of unfettered openness, there are three levels of foreign investment in China under a policy document known as *Catalogue Guiding Foreign Investment in Industry: Revision 2004*. The three categories, with varying restrictions, are *encouraged*, *allowed*, and *controlled*.[23] Telecom equipment falls under the encouraged category, according to which foreign vendors are allowed to compete freely and need not partner with Chinese companies, giving rise to the vigorous competitive position. But controlled investment, as the name suggests, restricts foreigners in sensitive areas, including transportation and shipping.

In the most visible example in the IT industry, despite China's accession to the World Trade Organization (WTO) in December 2001, investments in China's telecommunications carriers remain controlled. Restrictions include a requirement to partner with Chinese companies, a cap on the level of investment in fixed-line services (currently 25 percent but scheduled to rise to 49 percent in 2008), and restrictions on areas of operation and the types of services offered. In 2005 fixed-line service providers were allowed to operate in only three cities—Beijing, Guangzhou, and Shanghai—and only able to provide long-distance calls between these centers. On top of this, a long-awaited telecoms law was yet to be introduced, despite several years of debate. This raft of restrictions and uncertainty has effectively stalled foreign investment

INSTITUTIONS TO KNOW IN CHINA'S HIGH-TECH ECOSYSTEM

Over the past two decades, China has created a remarkable network, or ecosystem, for developing its rapidly growing information and communications technologies industries.

This well-evolved system has elevated China to the upper tier of global high-tech trade, placing it third, after the United States and Japan. In 2004, according to the Chinese Ministry of Commerce, China's high-tech import and export volume was approximately $330 billion, nearly 30 percent of its total foreign trade of $1.15 trillion.

Clearly China's influence in IT markets is great and increasing rapidly. Its high-tech foreign trade was on track to increase by 20 percent in 2006, to approximately $500 billion, according to Gartner estimates, after a 30 percent increase in 2005, to $416 billion.

Understanding the roles and relationships of key elements in the high-tech ecosystem provides obvious advantages for global buyers or merchants of IT products and services sourced from China.

The figure maps these key elements. Under the State Council, five ministries have direct influence on the shape and direction of research

China's high-tech ecosystem

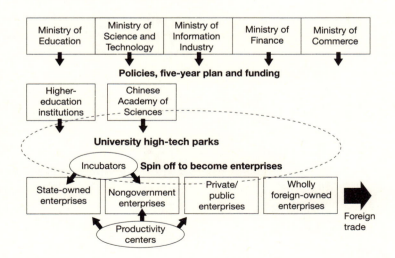

continued

and development, with the policy objective of advancing China's economic and social progress. Each is charged with setting strategies, guidelines, policies, and regulations in specific realms. The five ministries are:

- Ministry of Science and Technology (MOST)
- Ministry of Education (MOE)
- Ministry of Information Industry (MII), which oversees information and communications industries
- Ministry of Commerce (MOC), which oversees all commerce, with particular focus on science and technology
- Ministry of Finance (MOF), which oversees funding of the various ministries, R&D, and educational institutions based on priorities set by State Council directives

The National Development and Reform Commission (NDRC) and the State Assets Supervision and Administration Commission (SASAC) also are influential government agencies. The NDRC oversees planning and coordination of development across different industries. The SASAC controls all state-owned enterprises. A wise China strategy includes fostering good contacts and ongoing relationships with appropriate officials in these agencies.

Three other sets of institutions in the R&D network are the Chinese Academy of Sciences, government and private education institutions

in the area. The Chinese government is either the majority owner or the largest single shareholder of all six major telecommunications carriers.

State-owned enterprises (SOEs) can also distort commercial behavior. Directives to the telecom industry have included restrictions on the level of price competition allowable at a provincial level (it has been virtually eliminated), a ban on the use of mobile technologies in certain areas, and even changing the management structure within carriers (there was a major shake-up late in 2004).

from K1 through higher education, and four types of enterprise that generate high-tech economic production:

- **State-owned enterprises (SOEs).** These are mostly or wholly owned or closely controlled by central, provincial, or municipal governments.

- **Nongovernment enterprises (NGEs).** Known to the Chinese as *minying*, these domestic companies are spinoffs that are still partly owned by government agencies; they are allowed full autonomy in managing their profit/loss business similar to a private enterprise.

- **Private or public enterprises (PEs).** These are domestic companies that are in private or public ownership through shareholding.

- **Wholly foreign-owned enterprises (WFOE).** These are domestic companies wholly owned by foreign enterprises.

High-tech university parks and productivity centers round out the network. Park leaders commercialize promising research from nearby universities and Chinese Academy of Sciences institutes and create independent companies from promising campus research groups. Productivity centers transfer technology applications to small- and medium-sized businesses.

Source: Eng Chew, "Education, R&D Institutions Shaping the Chinese ICT Industry," G00138279, Gartner Research, April 13, 2006.

The friction between inflexible government regulations and fast-moving technologies can leave foreign companies vulnerable. Not only do laws change (the catalogue of foreign investors' guidelines is updated regularly), but companies can find themselves at odds with regulations as they adopt technologies seen as standard business practice in the West. Virtual private networks, connecting offices within China, are not yet a licensed service in China, and uncertainty remains about when (or if!) licenses will be formally issued.[24]

Standards

China is well aware of the need to foster its homegrown technological capabilities. Government efforts are not restricted to proclamations and speeches promoting a culture of innovation, or even stepped-up funding for science and technology. (See "Chinese Academy of Sciences: Leading Technology Research.")

In addition to foreign investment restrictions, the government has flexed its muscles in two main areas related to IT: standards and security. Each one has the potential to threaten, and even strangle, foreign

---

CHINESE ACADEMY OF SCIENCES: LEADING TECHNOLOGY RESEARCH

The Chinese Academy of Sciences (CAS) is respected and powerful in China's IT industry. Many of its current leaders have either received PhD's or have served as postdoctoral fellows in well-known Western universities and research institutions. They are actively recruiting foreign-trained Chinese research and development scientists, engineers, and managers. And they have initiated many joint research and exchange programs with foreign R&D institutions. The academy's goals for 2010 include:

- Becoming a national force for knowledge innovation—internationally recognized and geared for long-term success

- Having three to five CAS institutes acknowledged as world leaders in their selected fields

- Consistently producing successful high-tech startups as a highly efficient incubator for China's high-tech industry

- Becoming a national reservoir of science and technology talent, providing the knowledge and experts to grow the industry

Established in 1949, the CAS is the premier and largest research and education institution in China. With more than eighty R&D institutes, a university, and several graduate schools under its control, the

companies' aspirations in China. China has adopted a policy of setting its own technical standards in seven areas: wireless encryption, mobile telephony, alternative audio compression technologies, alternative video disc technologies, computer networking, multimedia applications on mobile telephones, and digital television. These standards have the potential to make market entry difficult for foreign companies offering products that use rival international standards.[25]

The supposed advantages of China's approach are a reduced reliance on foreign technology, reduced payments to foreign companies for their technology standards, a fostering of local industries through a de facto

---

CAS led China's pioneering steps in ICT. Its Beijing Institute of Computing Technology, in particular, is widely regarded as the founding force for China's ICT industry. To improve its ties with the industry, the CAS is charged with deriving its funding from government and business enterprises of all kinds. For this reason, we believe, its leaders increasingly are promoting an entrepreneurial culture.

The CAS promotes IT development in China in three ways:

- Conducting basic and applied research and achieving breakthrough innovations—including Chinese language processor and recognition systems, a supercomputer, and the dragon chip

- Educating experts to supply the CAS and other research institutes and industry enterprises—thirteen thousand students with six thousand PhD's awarded in 2001

- Supporting new business development by providing funding and resources to promising research projects and by transforming spinoffs into independent enterprises—with thirteen CAS institutions thus far converted into commercial enterprises, including Legend (the forerunner of Lenovo), Chinasoft, and Chengdu IT

Source: Eng Chew, "Education, R&D Institutions Shaping the Chinese ICT Industry," G00138279, Gartner Research, April 13, 2006.

protectionist barrier, and the availability of technology standards as a bargaining chip (see the section on "Security"). The lure of such an approach is clear. Chinese DVD manufacturers must pay the license holders of the DVD technology about $9 for each DVD sold. This becomes costly for Chinese manufacturers, which not only produce more than 10 million machines annually but also make a profit on individual machines priced as low as $12.[26] In its simplest form, the Chinese government's standards approach signals the move from rent payer to rent taker.

Despite standards initiatives gaining the original backing of Deng Xiaoping under the 863 program, the end results have been mixed. The mobile telephony standard, which was supposed to be a rival third-generation platform, is mostly owned by Nokia (32 percent), Ericsson (23 percent), and Siemens (11 percent). Even China Mobile and China Unicom appear likely to choose rival international standards ahead of the homegrown version. In this case, then, the government strategy appears to have resulted less in viable China technology standards and more in China gaining a say in the development of future technology standards.

Security

The Chinese government realized a similar gain when it adopted a wireless encryption standard known as wireless authentication and privacy infrastructure (WAPI), originally scheduled to be mandated in June 2004. If this regulation had gone into effect, no electronic product using a wireless local area network could be sold in China after that date without meeting the WAPI standard. As a result of protests by international vendors, implementation of the standard has been delayed indefinitely. By way of compensation, China has been offered a seat at the international standard-setting Institute of Electrical and Electronic Engineers (IEEE). China remains hopeful that WAPI will be included in the next wireless standard.

While this outcome can be seen as a softening of China's standards push (indicating a bias toward recommending standards rather than imposing them), foreign companies need be under no illusion about China's priorities when it comes to security issues. The WAPI standard was widely seen as little more than an attempt to introduce a domestic encryption standard that could be decrypted by the government.[27]

Foreign vendors ignore this focus on security at their peril. Internet monitoring by government and information censorship rules remain a constant of business life in China. In July 2004 China announced it had the capability to monitor text messages. The combination of government restrictions can have arcane effects: computer games developers are still a controlled form of investment in China, meaning foreign firms are simply barred from entry.

Piracy

The other issue that looms large for foreign IT executives considering China is the vulnerability of intellectual property (IP). Unfortunately, this also remains a constant of business life in China. In November 2003, in what was considered to be a landmark test case, Toyota lost a trademark infringement lawsuit against Chinese carmaker Geely. Toyota accused Geely of using a logo almost identical to Toyota's stylized *T* on its cars.[28] Digital piracy remains rampant. The Motion Picture Association of America estimates that 95 percent of movies sold in China are pirated. The World Bank has estimated that the United States would receive an additional $19 billion annually if it was paid royalties from IP breaches in developing countries.

While the piracy problem is severe, China is by no means inactive in this area. In fact, China has fallen victim to a good deal of mythmaking and a misunderstanding of historical trends. In recognition of China's efforts in this area, China was removed from the U.S. Trade Representative Priority Watch List in 1997 and has remained off the list ever since, while Taiwan and India, for example, still appear on the list.

As part of its accession to the WTO, China had to make significant changes to its IP protection policies, and twenty-three hundred regulations and laws have been repealed as a result of its membership. Moreover, the government has actively worked with vendors to enforce antipiracy laws (Nintendo has had considerable success in China, seizing more than 4.6 million products in eighty-five raids in 2003), successfully prosecuted breaches in court, and allowed foreign companies to file for trademark protection. Still, problems remain. While laws protecting IP exist, enforcement is uneven across the country. Nevertheless, most foreign companies regard the situation as improving.[29] We expect that WTO mandates will continue to be a positive force for economic reform, but that change will occur on an issue-by-issue basis, not as a wave of unforced government actions.

Historical Context

A focus on the aggrieved parties in IP violations has perhaps blinded most observers to the historical context for such violations. This context also provides a foundation for a much more positive view of China, which will be expanded in subsequent chapters.

Developing economies have regularly been profound violators of IP rights. This includes the United States in the nineteenth century: laws protected only the rights of U.S. citizens, allowing foreign works to be freely copied and sold. Charles Dickens toured the United States in 1842 because he was irritated that his *A Christmas Carol* was being sold there for six cents. This situation was not fully addressed for foreign authors until changes were made to U.S. law nearly one hundred forty years later—in 1981. Similar patterns can be seen in the progressive emergence of Japan, Taiwan, and South Korea, which all grew strongly in environments with initially weak IP protections.[30] Only when there has been more to be gained from IP protection—during the transition from rent payer to rent taker—has each jurisdiction adopted stringent laws.

China as an R&D Powerhouse

China is approaching the point where it may be advantageous to protect IP—including its own. It will come as a direct result of its standing not just as a low-cost manufacturer but as an innovative R&D power-house. While the current performance of its hardware and software industries allows a bleak assessment, there are trend lines pointing the right way. China's spending on R&D as a proportion of gross domestic product has climbed from .63 percent in 1995 to 1.23 percent in 2002. This is approaching Organisation for Economic Co-operation and Development levels of spending, which was 2.3 percent in 2001.[31] In terms of overall dollars, China made up 10 percent of global R&D spending in 2003, putting it third, behind the United States and Japan.

Another leading indicator of China's potential for innovation is the country's growing number of scientific papers listed on the Science Citation Index. In 1980 China published only 924 papers. By 2000 that had grown to 22,000, putting it ninth on the list. During the same period India's publications fell from 14,980 to 12,120.[32] This rise is being fueled by the incredible manpower and government resources China is bringing to bear on its IT industry. Despite reservations about quality, China graduated 2 million technicians and engineers in 2003. This volume allows for problems to be solved by sheer weight of numbers.

The government's long-awaited funding blueprint for science and technology, officially titled the *National Planning Outline for the Middle- and Long-Term Science and Technology, 2006 to 2020*, is nominally an impressive commitment of public and private resources. Prime Minister Wen Jiabao, a visible advocate for science-based development, chaired twenty teams of more than two hundred scientists who developed the innovation priorities over three years, with several revisions along the way. The stated objective is to build a "national innovation system" over the next fifteen years that can carry China to world-class stature in science and technology.

Can it work? Will it work? On the plus side, China's leaders are more unified than their counterparts in most Western nations in embracing technology as a strategic tool for national development. They are building a talent base with many Chinese ex-pats with several years' experience in technology hothouses in Silicon Valley or leading U.S. technology academies as well as the three hundred thousand engineers graduating each year from China's universities. While we agree with the McKinsey estimate that only 10 percent of the engineering graduates are qualified to step immediately into global corporations, we expect that the numbers of China's highest-quality engineering talent will increase in the years ahead. Indeed, the McKinsey analysis states that if China can raise the capabilities of its engineering graduates to the same level as India's today, China would have the largest pool of qualified young engineers in the world by 2008.[33]

On the negative side, China's attempt to mandate innovation in specific sectors, with its bias toward big science programs, defies the logic and often unpredictable nature of innovation. Several Chinese scientists teaching at U.S. universities said that they were disappointed by the lack of funding for basic research in the government's fifteen-year plan. Others noted that the emphasis on major programs would make it harder for scientists to pursue interests that are less visibly significant today but could overtake well-funded areas in terms of global impact five or ten years from now. Some stressed that big projects inevitably generate waste and corruption.[34]

The immense resources focused by the government and leading universities on technology development have created huge stakes for China's best-known researchers. Many stand to reap lavish financial gains from the companies they have helped to create and direct. But failure, especially when it involves fraud, can bring high costs as well. When the government determined in 2006 that a celebrated young scientist at Jiaotong University in Shanghai had faked research and copied designs for high-speed digital signal processing computer chips from a company in the West, it caused a national scandal. There remains "enormous pressure" on Chinese scientists to create world-class computer chips.[35]

Not Yet a Global Force in Computer Chips

Ultimately, China's huge population and rising living standards and the expertise its semiconductor industry develops in serving its home market will enable China to become more of a threat to global computer chip manufacturers. This will take several years, however.[36]

Gartner has projected China's total share of worldwide computer chip production capacity by year-end 2006 at only 6 percent. This was less than each of the world's two leading chip foundries, Samsung and Taiwan Semiconductor Manufacturing Company (TSMC), and only slightly more than the third largest, Intel.

China's leading chip makers compete mainly on price in lower-margin mature products, and we expect little change through 2010. Unless capital investments are accelerated overall and key innovations are achieved, China will lag other established manufacturing regions in this period.

Yet China's semiconductor industry is in its infancy. It has come a long way in technical proficiency and production capacity in a short time. Considering TSMC's rapid ascent since its founding across the Taiwan Strait in 1987, it would be a mistake to underestimate the mainland's global potential in chip production. TSMC is the world's largest dedicated semiconductor foundry and one of the world's top ten makers of integrated circuits.

The most likely Chinese candidate for long-term impact is Shanghai-based Semiconductor Manufacturing International Corporation (SMIC), China's leading wafer foundry and a standard-bearer for the country's high-tech industry. The company's revenues were just over $1 billion in 2005, and in mid-2006 orders were on the rise from "emerging" domestic customers as well as from overseas customers aiming to build their business in China.

SMIC also showed progress in advanced production methods. The global industry's state-of-the-art chip production plants in 2006 were producing wafers with 300-millimeter (12-inch) diameters. Intel operates four of these advanced plants in the United States. SMIC has one, in Beijing, which shipped its first commercial chips in spring 2006.

SMIC's founder and chief executive, Richard Ru-Gin Chang, holds a PhD in electrical engineering from Southern Methodist University, in Dallas. Before establishing SMIC in 2000, he had twenty years' experience at Texas Instruments. At TI, Dr. Chang built and managed technology development and operations of ten semiconductor fabrication plants and integrated circuit operations around the world.

Innovation investment is moving steadily east from its former capital of Silicon Valley. In the second half of 2005, companies that announced new or expanded investments in China included Alcatel, Intel, HP, Symantec, IBM, Nokia, Infosys, and Microsoft. In 1994 there were only seven majority-owned U.S. affiliates conducting R&D work in China. By 2000 there were 518.[37] In 2004 there were an estimated 750 R&D centers operating within China.

Investments in China in general, and some investments in China's IT market in particular, are exhibiting some of the characteristics of a bubble. Yahoo!'s $1 billion investment in business-to-business Web site Alibaba will probably be seen in hindsight as highly speculative.

But the seismic and long-lasting effects of China's emergence are already being felt. In low-cost manufacturing, the "China price" will continue to create disruption for manufacturers the world over as they seek to meet the challenges created by China's factories. The China price has come to mean the absolute lowest price available in the global market for mass-produced goods.

By 2008 it is highly likely that China will generate IP at a rate comparable to developed countries and, in the same year, actually surpass the United States as the population with the largest English-language capacity. (In terms of English language comprehension and proficiency, however, China will remain a challenger, not the global leader.) We anticipate that by 2010 at least eight Chinese IT brands will be recognized internationally.

To sum up, the world will witness the birth of a real IT superpower if government restrictions are loosened and the Chinese instinctive talent for entrepreneurialism continues to be encouraged. The next chapter assesses the likely paths China could take—and what we believe is the most likely outcome.

three

Charting the Course
for China to 2012

THE LEVEL OF government involvement in the Chinese economy is profound and in many ways unique in the world, given China's immense population and geography. The size and expected growth rate of the Chinese economy in coming decades will create one of the world's most significant accelerations in supply and demand for IT products and services.

Forecasting the pace and quality of world-class innovation within China is a much bigger question. Whether China emerges by 2012 as a global leader in science and technology innovation relevant for the information and communications technology (ICT) industry is a pivotal issue for business strategists and IT decision makers in Western corporations. China's success or failure in this regard will influence which global suppliers can establish a strong presence in China for the long haul and which of China's strongest domestic companies can compete in international markets.

The future of China's IT industry may not be clear for several years. Yet with potential rewards from engagement in China so high and the risks of staying on the sidelines potentially great, Western decision makers need to address these questions now. This chapter presents a framework for tracking the range of significant milestones and signposts most likely to affect planning and operations for IT buyers and vendors in China by 2012.

The three possible scenario paths charted in figure 3-1 summarize our view of the realistic range of outcomes. They may be characterized as follows:

1. *Isolation/Protectionism.* China's central government reverses some liberalizing actions of the past twenty-five years, as national economic growth slows, along with improvements in living standards: China retreats moderately from the global economy.

2. *Entrepreneurial.* The central government ownership of private assets substantially declines, as the economy sustains above-average rates of growth, with increased productivity and living standards: market forces increasingly determine domestic business activities.[1]

3. *China Inc.* The central government continues to embrace capitalist market incentives gradually, as the economy sustains above-average rates of growth and rising living standards: the government encourages higher levels of private sector innovation and investment.

To help Western decision makers map the directions China's ICT industry may take during the next five years, we provide a set of specific milestones to monitor events in relation to each of the three scenario paths. Gartner's methodology for mapping scenarios provides that for each milestone there must be a set of signposts that interested parties can observe and record as they plot their course through time. An ongoing focus on the milestones and signposts as they unfold in China also reduces dependence on official government or other public pronouncements. Generally the signposts will be specific measures related to the milestone or will signal the achievement or lack of achievement of the milestone.

FIGURE 3-1

China s ICT landscape in 2012

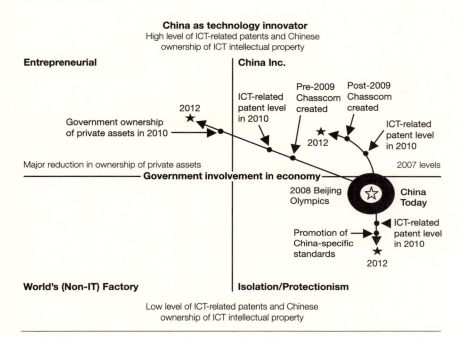

Consider the two-by-two matrix in figure 3-1 on which we plot the possible trajectories for China's ICT industries through 2012.[2] Strategists should monitor the events we highlight as signposts, which indicate accumulating momentum toward a given milestone, as they appear along the spectrum of possibilities for two critical uncertainties in China's future. The first uncertainty is the level of government involvement in the economy as measured by government ownership of private assets. The second is the level of innovation in science and technology as measured by patents in China related to information and communications technologies and China's ownership of intellectual property in these industries.

Focusing on these two dynamics cannot yield definitive answers, but they do help to define a range of outcomes. The horizontal axis in figure 3-1 spans a wide range for the Chinese government's future involvement in the economy: involvement is extremely low on the far left and very high on the far right. Similarly, the vertical axis spans a wide range of China's future stature as an innovator in science and technology in ICT products and services. Innovation is scored as very high at the top of the vertical axis and very low at the bottom.

Critical Uncertainty One: Government Involvement

Certainly there are multiple dimensions to many levels of Chinese government involvement in the economy at state, regional, and city levels. For our analysis, we believe that government ownership of private assets is the best measure for evaluating changing government involvement in the ICT industries. Government ownership of private assets directly affects private vendors in these industries, overwhelming most other market forces. The horizontal axis in figure 3-1 represents existing levels in 2007 on the far right and a major reduction in government ownership of private assets at the far left.

The current level of China's government involvement in the economy is more extensive than many business strategists and Western decision makers realize or expect. In our experience, the typical Western view of government involvement is that the Chinese government still owns many factors of production through state-owned enterprises (SOEs) and through unified Chinese Communist Party control of economic policies regulating both the national economy and individual companies.

The reality is both more complicated and more extensive. For this reason, we place the star representing China Today near the high end of the government involvement spectrum, on the far right. Most Chinese companies designated as "private" still retain some form of relationship with government officials or Chinese Communist Party members.

Consider the high-profile case of Huawei, the dominant brand within China for routers and other telecommunications equipment and an icon of China's private sector achievement and ambition. Huawei seems certain to upend Cisco Systems soon as the lead supplier overall in China. In addition to nearly one thousand patents in hand, Huawei has eight thousand patent applications pending on devices such as wireless terminals, fiber-optic switches, and data-routing systems. The company has seventeen thousand engineers and is spending about 10 percent of its annual revenues of R&D. The Chinese government seems committed to Huawei's continued success. In 2005 a state-owned Chinese bank extended a massive $10 billion line of credit to Huawei.[3]

Huawei is privately held, and the ownership structure is not known. It is rumored that Huawei was organized and developed by the Chinese military and is managed today by generals in the Chinese army. The generals presumably had, and have, strong interests in military capabilities and applications of advanced telecom systems.

For this reason, when considering partnering with or ordering equipment from Huawei, global strategists need to assess whether the company's presumed connection with the Chinese military might affect their business activities. The Indian government, for example, recently underscored this factor when it expressed national security concerns over Huawei's bid for some local telecommunication infrastructure projects in India.

In another example of government's strong ties to private companies, the city of Shanghai owns more than seven hundred companies, either entirely or fractionally, with an equity value of more than $16 billion and more than eight hundred thousand employees, according to some local reports.[4] The city also has partnership stakes in high-profile joint ventures with large, global multinational corporations. Shanghai GM, for instance, is a joint venture of General Motors Corporation and a wholly owned business of the Shanghai government, the Shanghai Automotive Industry Corporation (SAIC). Is it any surprise that the most popular vehicles sold in Shanghai are the line of cars under GM's Buick brand? Overall, General Motors was the second-largest carmaker in China, after Volkswagen, in the first half of 2006. Its passenger car sales increased 49 percent in the period, exceeding the 44 percent rate of increased sales overall in the first five months of the year for the auto industry in China. Major factors were declining prices and rising consumer confidence, especially in second-tier cities.[5]

That is good news for GM of course. Imagine the difficulties that other auto manufacturers with no state-owned partnerships could face when competing against rivals with a significant government-controlled ownership stake somewhere in their Chinese corporate structure? The government can and does easily influence distribution channels and operating costs through regulations, licensing requirements, and even direct financial aid.

Global partners can experience unexpected changes in control when partnering with an entity of the Chinese government. In early 2006, for example, Citibank was the second-largest shareholder of the Shanghai Pudong Development Bank, with a recently increased equity stake of 19.9 percent, the maximum allowed at the time under Chinese law. However, a group of six individual bank shareowners then sold their interests to a state-owned investment firm, thereby putting the Shanghai government and that investment firm ahead of Citibank's holding. Shanghai Pudong Development Bank is China's second-largest publicly traded banking company.[6]

A few months later China's bank regulator refused to permit a Citigroup-led consortium to acquire 85 percent of the troubled Guangdong Development Bank. In broad terms, Citigroup's consortium was competing with another group led by France's Société Générale SA for the opportunity to take management control of a Chinese bank and accelerate its pursuit of vast consumer lending opportunities in China. Yet a final regulatory decision, anticipated by the end of 2006, was likely to limit any foreign investment to less than 25 percent, essentially a junior position for setting strategic and operating priorities relative to domestic state-controlled owners.[7]

The lesson to be gleaned from these examples is that business planning is more challenging and likely outcomes less predictable in China because of the power and influence of multiple regulatory regimes. The best analyses and assumptions can be dashed with the stroke of a regulatory pen.

A second misconception that Western business strategists and IT executives often have about the Chinese Communist Party (CCP) is that it is a unified, consistent, and monolithic presence at all levels and geographic regions of the Chinese economy. This perception is somewhat accurate at the national level. There is only one structure for the CCP, and its actual membership is quite small—a few million members out of a total population of 1.3 billion. Yet national party unity breaks down very quickly at the level of city government, where opinions and motives often stray quite substantially from official national party lines.

Consider software exporting, for example. Competitive jostling among companies and supporting government networks in Beijing, Shanghai, Dalian, Shenzhen, Xian, and Chengdu is vehement, vocal, and persistent. This is typical in China. Career trajectories of leading party officials often fluctuate along with the social and economic fortunes of their cities. Things would be simple if it were a matter of effective positioning when financial incentives are on the line. But competition among Chinese cities involves more than money. Party status and influence within the national Communist Party is always at stake.

To accommodate these political realities, we offer the following suggestions:

- Establish separate offices for your wholly foreign-owned enterprise (WFOE), your wholly owned Chinese company, and your representative office. Some issues are best handled with government officials through your WFOE and some through your representative office. The dual-investment can prove valuable over time.

- Develop relationships with government officials of the same agency in different cities where you do business. For example, if you have operations in Beijing and Shanghai, have good contacts at the National Development and Reform Commission in Beijing as well as at the National Development and Reform Commission in Shanghai.

- Do *not* allow yourself to be caught in the middle of intercity, regional-central, and interministry government disputes. This is rarely as easy as it sounds. One Western firm wisely avoided upsetting officials in different cities competing to host a high-profile company event by having a central government agency or ministry make the decision. The city officials accepted the choice. But officials at central government ministries who were not asked to participate were rankled.

Critical Uncertainty Two: China as a Technology Innovator

Governments in every developed economy play important roles in supporting innovation. Clearly this is true on many levels in China as well. Yet the government's ownership of private companies, its continued tolerance or limited effectiveness in curbing piracy of intellectual property, and its active hand in directing capital flows (through direct budget allocations or control of lending policies at Chinese banks) all restrict competition.

When market forces are restricted, incentives to innovate through risk taking are dampened, for market signals are key drivers of innovation. They indicate where opportunity for innovation is particularly attractive, such as in pricing, product and service features, or distribution channels. They also indicate how much innovation is needed, letting would-be innovators assess investment trade-offs between creating new features and getting features into the market ahead of competitors.

In recent years China has made some progress in IP creation and international patents—the metrics we believe best measure a nation's progress in generating innovation. And there is significant opportunity for China to accelerate its global standing in innovation, given major investments under way at institutions of higher education, science, and technology and in related commercial industrial parks.

Chinese companies face many challenges related to innovation: lack of experience in international marketing, competition from foreign providers, and, not to be overlooked, competition within China from local competitors that have the advantages of what amount to extensive subsidies from government agencies. The six cities just noted, China's centers of software development for export, have made enormous investments in their local companies and continue to support many of them with easy credit and other forms of cash and bureaucratic aid.

From a capitalist's perspective, these forms of government support are so extensive that they seriously distort market forces. Companies are not allowed to succeed or fail based on merit and competitive advantage. This protection from failure penalizes the more efficient companies. Over time, the survival of weak competitors is a serious disincentive to the entrepreneurial risk taking required to drive innovation. When it is difficult to see economic Darwinism at work—survival of the fittest—it is difficult to encourage industrial innovation.

Yet there will be innovation in China. It will happen differently than in the West, but it will happen. The government often acts as a winnowing force, picking winners in a race to the top. If a company has been truly innovative, perhaps in operations or distribution if not technology, and growing its business, then it is apt to find favor with government ministers in terms of funding, regulatory advantages, and networking opportunities. We have observed this repeatedly.

Western strategists and decision makers must be aware of how Chinese government officials regard Chinese companies that become or are potentially important elements in your China strategy. Government-conferred resources and honors obviously are favorable signs. Another obvious caution, worth repeating here, is to be wary at all times of Chinese partners with the potential to become future competitors. Chinese companies are always eager to learn whatever they can from Western partners. Technology, capital, process design—the pursuit is relentless.

There are many positive aspects to economic development activities that support China's ICT industries. But government ownership of private companies, government's continued tolerance of IP piracy, and active government participation in bank-lending policies all conspire to limit innovation, which could greatly enhance the national economy.

Microsoft's cautious government partnerships in China are a case in point. Beijing has promoted the joint venture of Tata Consultancy Services (TCS), the National Development Reform Commission (NDRC), and Microsoft and is very supportive of Microsoft's Haidian District development laboratories. Microsoft praises the brilliance of Chinese scientists it employs there. But most benefits from truly innovative work these developers generate in China are built into products and services that Microsoft is very reluctant to sell in China. Put bluntly, Microsoft is exporting world-class Chinese creativity derived from its investments there in expectation of higher returns on investment outside China.

Of course, by its own estimates, Microsoft has been a victim of pirated IP in China since it first entered the market in the early 1990s. The company estimates that perhaps 90 percent of its branded Windows and Office applications used in China are stolen—pirated by copiers who distribute and sell the programs at a fraction of their market value. Until official crackdowns on IP piracy are accelerated, Microsoft will have few incentives to innovate specifically for the Chinese market.

President Hu Jintao knows this problem for Microsoft has negatives as well for China. On his 2006 visit to Microsoft's headquarters in Redmond, Washington, Hu hailed Microsoft chairman Bill Gates as "a friend of China" and vowed to accelerate the government's efforts to combat piracy.[8] This will take many years to achieve, but real action was evident a few weeks prior to Hu's face-to-face meeting with Gates. The Chinese government required that all computer manufacturers in the country install operating systems during assembly. Three of its biggest PC makers—Founder Technology Group, TCL Group, and Tsinghua Tongfang—then committed to three-year deals, valued collectively at $420 million, for licenses to Microsoft Windows. They followed China's biggest PC maker, Lenovo, which was already on record to spend about $150 million in 2006 on Windows software for computer sales in China. The payments represented "a milestone achievement," according to Craig Mundie, Microsoft's chief technical officer, who added that continued government reform on software piracy "still has a long distance to go."[9]

As the world's factory, China produces technology products that rely on large numbers of workers to assemble and package goods. The import market is strong, but the Taiwanese, Korean, and Japanese companies that rely on Chinese suppliers for hardware and software are very cautious about how much intellectual capital they share with

China and what, if any, proprietary technologies they transfer to their Chinese suppliers or partners. The Chinese provide a production arena for cheaper, faster, and smaller goods, but rarely are they smarter and more innovative.

Indeed, there is a risk that China's international position will decline if its ambitions to become a global leader in science and technology do not succeed. This could happen if the Chinese government does not accelerate its disinvestment of private assets or, worse, if the government halts or reverses its gradual liberalization of the controlled economy. Reality in 2012 will likely fall somewhere in the middle. There will be a continuing gradual withdrawal by the government as an equity owner in the economy. For this reason, we see China's ability to innovate improving at very modest levels.

Milestone One: Beijing 2008 Summer Olympic Games

A sporting event might seem an odd choice for business strategists to put high on their list of planning priorities. But in the case of global IT companies and China, the Beijing 2008 Summer Olympics, scheduled for August 8–24, is a singular event. It is highly likely to have economic and political repercussions within China and for its relations with the outside world.

The preparations, execution, and results of the Beijing Olympics will be closely followed in corporations, think tanks, and academic institutions for hints of future policy leanings by the Chinese Communist Party. An extensive monitoring of the economic and political dimensions of the games should be part of strategists' business analysis regarding policies, opportunities, and threats that impinge on the global IT industry in China.

In figure 3-1, we illustrate the importance of the Olympics milestone with the wide band encircling the star that represents China Today. The thick width is meant to convey an extended period of time before outcomes and implications of the games emerge. Preparations began in earnest shortly after Beijing was selected to host the 2008 games in 2001. And the Chinese appear genuinely to have embraced these Olympics with fervor. Anticipation and excitement is reinforced by daily reports and updates in state-controlled media. The games have been an extremely high priority for party leaders, influencing budget and policy debates and international diplomacy. We expect that by the opening of the annual National People's Congress in the Great Hall of the People at Tiananmen Square in 2009, party leaders will have determined which of the three paths outlined in this chapter they want China to travel in coming years.

A successful Olympics could encourage party leaders to continue, or perhaps accelerate, gradual political and economic liberalization reforms. In the eyes of party leaders, a successful Olympics would include well-staged sporting competitions; restrained and effective police response to anticipated pro-Taiwan, pro-democracy, and other demonstrations or terrorist threats; and broadly positive global news coverage of China's social, economic, and cultural progress.

However, clashes in the streets that result in bloodshed and deaths, outbreaks of military conflict with Taiwan, elevated trade disputes with the United States or Japan, or operational breakdowns that embarrass the Chinese leaders could lead to a policy backlash. Party leaders might conclude pre-Olympic liberalization steps had gone too far. With more than twenty thousand foreign journalists expected to be out of the country by September, police and legal crackdowns could be more easily planned and carried out then.

Some skeptical observers in China believe that party leaders have been on their best behavior, more accommodative to global sentiment on China's foreign and domestic policies, in order to promote a positive atmosphere for diplomacy and its global reputation prior to the Olympics. But, these skeptics warn, the government will revert to more confrontational and isolationist activities in the aftermath of the games.

Clearly the Chinese government has not backed down in some disputes with the West. The *New York Times* accused the Beijing government of unjustly jailing one its Chinese researchers because they suspected that he had provided closely guarded state secrets about imminent changes in party leadership that the newspaper published in 2004. Charges against the reporter, which the *Times* denied, were dropped prior to President Hu Jintao's April 2006 visit to the White House and reinstated after Hu's return to Beijing. The state secrets charge was thrown out by a Beijing court four months later, but the judges sentenced the Chinese journalist to three years on an unrelated fraud charge. His jail term, including time served prior to the conviction, was scheduled to end in September 15, 2007.[10]

The episode "should be another signal to global corporations that the rule of law in China is still little more than a handy slogan," the newspaper said in an editorial prior to the ruling.[11] Thus the possibility of a retreat into isolation/protectionism and of increased government involvement in the Chinese economy after the Olympics is not out of the question. Global IT strategists and decision makers must be aware of and plan for these contingencies.

Writing in the autumn of 2006, we remain cautious optimists. Of the three potential paths we depict in figure 3-1, a move into the China Inc. quadrant is by far the most likely, characterized by gradual improvements in innovation and a gradual decline in government ownership stakes in the private economy. We rate the likelihood of this outcome a 70 on a scale of 100. We rate the entrepreneurial path a 20 and the isolation/protectionism path just 10 on a scale of 100.

For the Chinese people, the Beijing Summer Olympics is a focal point of enormous national pride. The date selected for the Opening Ceremony, August 8, 2008, or 8-8-08, has a culturally auspicious meaning for the Chinese. The number eight in Mandarin is pronounced "ba" and sounds similar to the Cantonese word *fa,* which means "fortune." This is a historic opportunity not only for Chinese athletes to seriously challenge the United States, Russia, and other nations in front of cheering crowds for most medals won, but also for China to assert its role as a world-leading nation of the twenty-first century. "We want to convey the image of a China that is more open and that is making progress," Jiang Xiaoyu, executive vice president of the Beijing Organizing Committee for the 29th Olympic Games (BOCOG), told reporters at the 2006 Winter Olympics in Turin, Italy.[12]

This should not be difficult. The urban renewal we have seen in Beijing, spurred by Olympics spending, has been dramatic and impressive since 2002. The Chinese government has budgeted an estimated $30 billion preparing for the games. Global marketers including GE, Johnson & Johnson, Lenovo, Panasonic, and Samsung, and leading Chinese brands, including Bank of China, China Mobile, and Sinopec have signed up as sponsors.

These corporations are paying for the rarified opportunity the games provide to network with China's most influential business and political leaders. They also hope to link their brands emotionally, and favorably, to what they obviously have wagered will be a powerful, uplifting event for the Chinese people. GE said it hopes to double its revenues in China to $10 billion in 2008. "The Olympics is one way we can speed up the process," said GE executive Peter Foss.[13]

To gauge the Olympics' potential positive impact for China's stature in the world and economic gains at home, consider these facts:

- An estimated 250,000 foreign tourists, including visitors coming specifically for the games as well as regular tourists traveling to China, are expected in Beijing during the games. Beijing expects to add 110 new hotels for a total of 800, expanding accommodations during the games to 550,000 people a day, according to the Beijing Tourism Bureau.[14]

- The Olympics is the largest media event in the world, with news coverage spanning the globe. The Beijing Organizing Committee estimates that more than 21,600 accredited media—16,000 broadcasters and 5,600 press and photographers representing over 200 countries—will be in China.[15] Most will be reporting on sporting events, but many will be fanning out across the city and country to tell stories about the people, politics, and life in modern China.

- Anticipated benefits to Beijing's economy include 1.8 million new jobs and improved transportation, housing, infrastructure, sporting facilities, and environmental standards.[16]

"We not only strive to stage a high-level distinguishing Olympic Games, but also . . . to push forward the economic development and raise the level of people's living conditions," Jiang of the BOCOG told the Japanese newspaper *Yomiuri Shimbun*. Living standards for Beijing citizens had already improved as a result of preparations for the Olympics, he said.[17]

In addition to the Olympics milestone for 2008, we have identified four other milestones for the ICT industry:

- China's patent performance related to information and communications technologies

- Progress toward creating an effective national marketing and trade organization, modeled on India's respected and effective National Association of Software and Services Companies (NASSCOM), to manage and promote the interests of China's ICT industries in public policy discussions and international affairs

- Levels of Chinese government ownership of private assets

- Promotion of China-specific standards

Some of these milestones appear in more than one of the scenario paths charted in figure 3-1. This is because the signposts at each milestone can lead in different directions depending on which choices are made when and which opportunities are taken or missed.

Milestone Two: Patent Performance in Information and Communications Technology

ICT-related patent performance is a highly valuable measure of China's capability for technology innovation, indicating both the direction China is moving in and specific measures to use as signposts through 2012. In 2006 China's patent performance in ICT shows signs of very strong momentum, with a few significant areas of concern.

Patent data is difficult to obtain with consistency from the three major patent offices: European Patent Office (EPO); U.S. Patent and Trademark Office (USPTO); Japan Patent Office (JPO); and the Chinese State Intellectual Property Office (SIPO). However, the 2005 report from the Organization of Economic Cooperation and Development (OECD) contains extensive information from the EPO, including China's ICT-related patent performance in Europe.[18] We recommend that strategists and decision makers use this and similar reports to determine China's patent position in 2007 and subsequent years.

ICT Patents as a Percentage of Total Patents

This is the first measure to examine from the EPO. In 2002 China ranked fifth, at 45 percent, ahead of Japan, the United States, the European Union, and the worldwide average. China trailed only Singapore, Korea, Finland, and the Netherlands—countries that are home to highly innovative companies, including Philips, Samsung, Nokia, and many significant semiconductor manufacturers.

Specialization Index

The OECD also calculates a specialization index (SI) for ICT-related patents. This measure is calculated as the share of ICT-related patents a country files at the EPO, divided by the share of that country's patent filings with the EPO in all technology areas. When the SI value of ICT-related patents is greater than one, the country has a higher share in ICT-related patents relative to its share in all technology areas. Conversely, when the SI value of ICT-related patents is below one, the country has a lower share in ICT-related patents than in all technology areas combined. In 2002 China was ranked tenth, with an SI value just over one—more than double China's 1995 rank in the specialization index.

These first two signposts clearly indicate what anyone following China's economic advancements of the past decade would expect: China's momentum in technology innovation is growing. However, we need to consider three additional signposts that collectively raise questions of whether China will encounter increasing constraints in innovation capacity in the 2007–2012 period.

Foreign Ownership of Domestic ICT-Related Inventions

For China, the 2000–2002 average was approximately 50 percent—a very high percentage but not uncommon for developing economies. It suggests of course that half of the patented inventions being generated in China in this period were funded and directed by companies outside China. As one would expect, leading Western economies have much lower percentages of foreign-owned inventions. The United States reported 15 percent; the European Union, 15 percent; and Japan, only 2 percent.

ICT-Related Patents with Foreign Coinventors

China's average in 2000–2002 was approximately 30 percent. Clearly the contribution of foreign collaborators is an important part of the innovation story in China. The United States and the European Union appear to be good role models in free trade and cross-border collaboration, but their respective percentages in this category are only 15 percent and 10 percent. The worldwide average is only 5 percent. Once again, as expected, considering its well-known insularity, Japan has little foreign collaboration in this category: its average was only 2 percent.

Domestic Ownership of ICT-Related Inventions Made Abroad

For China, the 2000–2002 average was approximately 20 percent. This is very close to the U.S. average of 19 percent and the worldwide average of 18 percent. Yet we would expect a lower percentage. Isn't China supposed to be the manufacturing location of choice? The European Union has only 10 percent of its ICT-related inventions manufactured abroad. The Japanese control their ICT IP even more tightly, with only 5 percent manufactured abroad.

Milestone Three: A National Trade Association to Promote China's ICT Industry

When you meet with government officials and representatives of Chinese high-tech parks, invariably these officials say that their city really has the advantage within China in the ICT industry. You will hear about their city's large, fast-growing, dynamic, and cutting-edge capabilities. And you will also hear that every other city with comparable productive capacity is bad, unqualified, and unworthy.

This intense intercity rivalry is related to the structure of the CCP itself. This lack of cohesion flows from the political arena into businesses that are leading China's advances in information and communications technologies. As a result, the industry has been its own worst enemy. It has not created the marketing sophistication required to build global competitors. And it has not developed persuasive unified messages for educating and persuading government trade officials on the benefits to Chinese companies available in freer trade and capital markets.

The solution is no mystery. The Chinese ICT industry has no further to look than India for the right model to correct these failings. India's National Association of Software and Services Companies, widely known as NASSCOM, is the national chamber of commerce for India's software and services industry. Moreover, it is an effective national and global advocate for the industry, with more than nine hundred member companies. Among other industry priorities, NASSCOM campaigns for tough enforcement by India's government bureaucracy of IP rights. And it trumpets the world-class capabilities of its members, serving as the industry's comprehensive marketing bazaar.

The NASSCOM Web site (www.nasscom.org) provides a wealth of descriptive and introductory information for potential customers and collaborators anywhere in the world. Here's a sampling of promotional headlines taken from the site:

- "India's IT Industry Opposes Caste Quotas"

- "Bangalore is Far From Saturated: Nasscom Chief"

- "Foreign Nationals Flock to Indian Multinationals"

- "India Gets Animated About Animation"

- "NASSCOM to Create Employee Registry"

One can imagine what such a collaboration, a "Chasscom" ("China Association of Software and Service Companies"), might achieve for China's ICT companies, especially those with potential for global success. (We use "Chasscom" here simply for the sake of discussion and do not necessarily recommend it as the proper name for such an organization in China or suggest that it necessarily be exactly patterned after India's NASSCOM.) Yet there are many obstacles that hinder the building of a Chasscom. The industry is currently divided about how to move ahead, and there is much squabbling about the appropriate organizational structure, membership, funding, management, and so on. An awakening of government interest is discernible, but mainly in Beijing.

Nonetheless, we take the long view and are optimistic that a Chasscom will be organized. Achieving this milestone would reflect a lessening of the Chinese government's involvement in the economy—a willingness to hand more control of the ICT industry to its owners and allies in private industry. As argued above, the establishment of a Chasscom on par with India's NASSCOM would provide a major lift to potential innovation that can arise within China's ICT industry.

Milestone Four: Government Ownership of Private Sector Assets

Our fourth milestone is government ownership of private assets. This is one of the more profound types of government involvement in the economy: it distorts government policy decisions and it reduces the effectiveness of market forces to drive industry growth through healthy and fair competition.

Milestone Five: Promotion of China-Specific Standards

Our final milestone is promotion of China-specific standards. This milestone will only appear should China slip into an isolation/protectionism stance either from a negative Beijing Olympic outcome or from some other significant retrenchment of China's global position.

Conclusion

The two biggest uncertainties in forecasting likely conditions in 2012 are the level of government involvement in the economy and the relative pace of China's ICT innovation in the world. Global companies—both users and providers of IT equipment and services—should focus on five milestones to forecast coming changes in government involvement and innovation capacity in China's ICT industry.

Identifying and responding to these changes strategically and rapidly will provide important competitive advantages. Aspiring early movers who apply these frameworks should have an edge in deciding how best to advance or establish business interests in China that engage markets and ecosystems of the ICT industry.

The five milestones bearing close scrutiny are: the Beijing 2008 Summer Olympics, patent performance in information and communications technology, creation of a national trade association to promote China's ICT industry (Chasscom), government ownership of private-sector assets, and promotion of China-specific standards. Careful tracking of signposts that define these milestones over the next five years will help global companies predict ICT market conditions in China long before the 2012 landscape is fully formed.

Our schematic presentation of milestones and possible outcomes (figure 3-1) defines three distinct potential paths: Entrepreneurial, Isolation/Protectionism, and China Inc. The China Inc. scenario represents a continuation of China's present course of gradual decline in government's role in the economy and ICT industry and modest gains for China in world-class innovation. We strongly believe that this is the most likely landscape for China's ICT industry in 2012. However, extremely positive or negative developments could happen at any of the four milestones. This would significantly change industry conditions, yielding either greater market-led dynamics (Entrepreneurial scenario) or a retreat into greater government control (Isolation/Protectionism scenario).

PART TWO

India

India

REALITY VERSUS PERCEPTION

THE PERSONAL columns in the *Times of India* provide an engaging account of what modern India has become: "Alliance invited from a well established business man or professional, preferably from Mumbai for intelligent, attractive well groomed software engineer, Maharashtrian girl, 26 . . . hailing from affluent business family and is into software consultancy and medical transcription business." Another says: "Alliance invited for Kshatriya Burud boy, 28 . . . software engineer in USA, arriving in December, from parents of fair graduate girl willing to go to USA."[1]

These personal postings suggest the focus on IT within India has become nothing less than a craze. In many ways, and especially for millions in India's younger generations, IT is India's national obsession. Each state attempts to designate its own "IT cities" and to present itself as an attractive location for IT. The projected image is sometimes feebly or naively done, yet it is convincing in locales where focused IT investments by the private sector and favorable government policies have taken root.

The image of India as a premier IT destination is enhanced by the strong performance of India's leading IT companies, such as Wipro Technologies, Infosys Technologies, and Tata Consultancy Services (TCS). Exports of IT services made up about 49 percent of India's total services exports, worth $25 billion in 2003–2004, growing at an annual rate of about 36 percent a year.[2]

Additionally there is tantalizing potential, as discussed in part III, for India's expertise in software and software services to fit well with China's expertise in hardware and manufacturing. A fundamental premise of this book is that alliances building on each country's complementary skills could create truly global IT behemoths, disrupting almost every other business in specific industry sectors.

But there are many hurdles to be overcome before this vision can be realized. Thus global strategists and decision makers would be ill-advised to take the hype at face value. Gartner evaluated the capabilities of twenty-nine cities across India with the demonstrated or stated desire to become a base for foreign IT companies.[3] Of these, sixteen had done little or nothing to achieve this goal, leaving prospective IT offshore companies facing difficulties as diverse as energy shortages, language barriers, limited access by air, religious strikes, and unsupportive governments. Only six of the twenty-nine—Bangalore, Mumbai, New Delhi, Chennai, Hyderabad, and Pune—could be recommended without reservation as locations for investments and sourcing partnerships by foreign companies.

These findings reflect the two gravest challenges to a continuation of the Indian IT industry's recent performance. First is the country's woefully inadequate infrastructure. Second is the capacity of India's reputed army of highly educated engineers to meet the growing demands of an IT industry aspiring to serve both international and domestic customers. Both challenges run counter to some common assumptions. Visitors to Mumbai, Bangalore, and New Delhi could be forgiven for thinking that, despite some modest discomfort, India's infrastructure and governance structures are up to the standards demanded of modern businesses. To put it bluntly, for reasons explained below, they are not. Similarly, much has been written in recent times about India's colleges turning out massive numbers of highly skilled science and engineering graduates. But this image of a limitless, English-literate workforce is not entirely accurate.

Diversity

Strategists and decision makers in global IT companies still assessing India as a destination for outsourcing, for a role in a global supply chain, or as a domestic market in its own right should view India as not one country but as several separate countries. India should be approached as a confederation of twenty-eight states and seven union territories (similar to the District of Columbia in the United States) that are held together successfully by one government. This proposition affects all the obvious factors that executives face when evaluating an area within India for a potential work site: training, language skills, governance, and infrastructure. But our argument goes further. Foreign strategists and decision makers need to understand and appreciate ethnic tensions, religious tensions, and social tensions between separate and starkly different communities, some of which have, even in recent times, been close to outright war. CIOs and managers with IT vendors active in India might wonder why we emphasize these issues. Quite simply, you must be aware of how local culture, politics, and traditions affect the motivation and living conditions of potential Indian employees, service providers, and product suppliers.

The personal story of one of the authors provides insight into the wide diversity of cultures and identities in India. Partha was born in Bangalore, in the southern state of Karnataka. His wife, Jhumkee, was born in Kolkata (Calcutta), nine hundred forty miles to the northeast, in the state of West Bengal, which borders Bangladesh. Their only common language is English, since their native states have separate official languages—Kannada and Bengali. India's Constitution recognizes twenty-two languages in the country, although the number of dialects is put as high as eight hundred fifty. Mirroring India's national profile, Karnataka and West Bengal are predominantly Hindu but have large numbers of Muslims. In India, 828 million identify themselves as Hindu, 138 million as Muslim, 24 million as Christian, 19 million as Sikh, 8 million as Buddhist, and 4 million as Jain.[4] There are even an estimated five thousand Jews in India, mainly in Mumbai.

If this were not dizzying enough, the state governments in Karnataka and West Bengal have very different political ideologies. The center-leftist

Congress Party, which led India to independence sixty years ago, dominates in Karnataka and is seen as the establishment party. The Communist Party, which controls the political structure in West Bengal, is widely
viewed as representing the interests of workers and lower caste members.

The practical effects of this diversity are omnipresent, right down
to the most basic level. "When I go to Kolkata I have no idea of what the
road signs or shop signs say," Partha says. "Many of our relatives don't
speak English. Diversity across India is often staggering to someone
who has looked at it from afar." Partha's personal story is one very simple example, but it deftly hints at deep differences along geographical,
linguistic, religious, political, and social lines within India.

This diversity—in terms of religious outlook, education, and location—has real effects on the standard and stability of the available
workforce. Some states, notably Gujarat, are regularly affected by religious strikes, known as *bandhs*. Thus business commitments in Gujarat
may be risky if the likely pool of employees is vulnerable to bandhs.

Regrettably, the sheer diversity and scale of India also overrides
some otherwise impressive statistics about India's education system.
On the face of it, India is well positioned to lead a shake-up of the
global information technology industry, with 90 million college-age students, compared with about 20 million in the United States.[5]

But the reality is somewhat different. Across India, 5,600 doctorates in science and technology were awarded in 1998–1999, the most
recent figure available. By comparison, the United States issued 27,100
doctorates in science and engineering in 2001, a moderate decline from
the peak in 1998.[6] About 44 percent of the adult population in India is
illiterate, a reasonable statistic when you recall that 60 percent of adult
Indians in 2006 worked in agriculture.[7] For perspective, consider that
farm workers in the United States last exceeded 60 percent of employed adults nearly a hundred years ago, just prior to World War I.

In a survey released in June 2005, McKinsey & Company found
that only one in four graduate engineers in India were suitable for employment in multinational companies, based on interviews with eighty-
three human resources professionals.[8] The figure dropped to 15 percent for finance or accounting graduates and 10 percent for those with

general degrees. "In India the overall quality of the educational system, apart from the top universities, could improve significantly," McKinsey concluded, in quite an understatement. It cited unnamed instances in which call centers had been relocated from India to the Philippines because of difficulties operators experienced in speaking English.

Concerns about standards of education have been voiced repeatedly within India as well. As we saw in chapter 3, the volume of published scientific articles is a leading indicator of future innovation driven by research and development. In comparing India's growth rate, Professor Subbiah Arunachalam of the M. S. Swaminathan Research Foundation found that India's slower pace in published articles contributed to his country being overtaken by China in 1996. Moreover, India's share of scientific articles published globally has been declining.[9]

Chapter 6 examines more closely this crucial question of available— and suitable—labor in relation to the development of India's IT industry. The key point here is that India is facing the seemingly absurd situation of labor shortages in key areas of IT. Companies targeting India's domestic market are showing a growing recognition of the challenges. In one small example, Intel is planning to offer eight Indian languages in its bundled software in a low-cost computer the chipmaker is developing for the Indian market at a cost of $250 million.

Cultural Background

The profound political movement in India in the past half century has been toward *emphasizing*, rather than overcoming, divisions along ethno-regional lines. Various "nationalist" political parties often pander to ethnic biases. It is unlikely, therefore, that religious rivalries and language differences will fade soon from India's modern business environment.

In the state of Gujarat, for example, English is not printed alongside Gujarati on official state forms—an enduring example of nationalist sentiment against Britain's colonial rule. More disturbingly, Hindu nationalist sentiment was forcibly expressed in the same state in 1992, when mobs destroyed the Muslim temple of Ayodhya. Muslims had built the temple on the supposed birthplace of the Hindu God Rama. At least a thousand people died in the subsequent rioting.

More recently, the Ayodhya temple issue flared in February 2002, after an attack on a train from the temple carrying Hindu religious volunteers. The New York–based Human Rights Watch blamed involvement by the Bharatiya Janata Party (BJP)—the Hindu nationalist party—for systematic retaliatory anti-Muslim pogroms in Gujarat. As a result, twenty-five hundred people died and an estimated one hundred thousand others were displaced.[10] The BJP was the dominant political party within India at the time, leading the national government from 1996 to 2004.

The message for businesses is clear: misunderstanding the local social, political, and religious context can be disastrous.

History

India owes its diversity to its richly layered history, which stretches back to the first major kingdom on the subcontinent, dating around the fourth century BCE. Despite thousands of years of recorded history, India as a nation is a relatively new concept. Until the mid-eighteenth century, India was dominated for two hundred years by the Mughal Empire, centered in northern India. But after that period, the central authority was challenged both internally and, from 1757, by the mercantile ambitions of the British East India Company. The British claimed sovereignty over India in 1858. But India was far from united under British rule.[11] Britain was only able to gradually expand its hold over India by forming treaties with individual Indian states that formed alliances with Britain to topple their neighbors. Even though Britain eventually exercised direct rule over most of the nation, in 1935 there were an estimated six hundred "princely states" that formally held sovereign power.[12] It was not until 1947 that the Congress Party won the independence of a united India—and even this was achieved only by ceding the creation of the predominantly Muslim nation of Pakistan, a decision accompanied by bloody riots and mass migrations.

Politics

Given the nation of India's relatively recent birth, it is perhaps little wonder that India still struggles with what appear to foreigners as threshold political issues. The domination of the Congress Party for more than forty years since 1947 independence was typified by an isolationist, protectionist approach to the economy with a strong leaning toward nationalized industries.[13] At the same time, the government protected and fostered powerful industrial interests to the extent that the so-called Bombay Club of industrialists is still known for its power and influence. For example, the Tata family, which grew its business by supplying rails to Britain during World War I, formed the basis of India's heavy industry after the war. Helped by protectionist policies, the group now includes Tata Steel, India's largest steel company; Tata Motors, India's largest car manufacturer; and TCS, one of India's largest software service providers.

India was shaken from its isolationist, protectionist stance in 1991 because of a payments crisis—the government was seriously overspending as reserves evaporated. To end the crisis, the government had to pledge its gold reserves with the International Monetary Fund (IMF) and obtain a huge loan. Only after this bitter experience did Indian leaders realize the importance of economic reform. The initial economic reform movement was led by Manmohan Singh, finance minister during the period and since 2004 prime minister of the Congress Party–led coalition government.

India Today

The wheels of economic reform turn slowly in India. India's protectionist past has resulted in a legacy of many layers of bureaucracy that can entangle any business endeavor—a situation known derisively within India as "the license raj." World Bank figures show that it takes 71 days to launch a business in India, compared with 48 days in China and 5 days in the United States. It takes 270 days to comply with permit and license requirements in India, compared with 363 days in China and 70 days in the United States.[14]

The current ambitious reform program of Singh's national government is also hampered by the fact that the government is a tenuous coalition. The stability of his ruling coalition government depends on the "support" of forty-three elected Communist Party parliamentarians. The necessary political accommodation that occurs within a democratic system is illustrated by Singh's program of privatizing national industries. In August 2005 Singh admitted the reform program had stalled due to the obstructionist positions of the Communists. These kinds of hurdles can occur throughout India, where state governments hold considerable power. The constitution gives states control over public order, welfare, health, education, local government, and industry.

Historians openly discuss the criminalization of India's political system since the 1970s, pinpointed as occurring during Indira Gandhi's term as prime minister and continuing at every level of the political system today. Well-reported scandals include the payments of commissions in the Bofors arms deal that tainted Rajiv Gandhi's administration in 1987 and the diversion of government money meant for animal husbandry to senior party officials, which led to former Bihar Chief Minister Laloo Prasad Yadav being jailed repeatedly in the late 1990s.

The party founded by Yadav, the Rashtriya Janata Dal, is one of the key coalition members of the current national government. Yadav is now railways minister. His party was only thrown out of government in Bihar in the 2005 November elections.[15] Unfortunately, a criminal taint extends to all levels. In the 2004 state elections the Karnataka Election Watch committee discovered that candidates in 91 of 104 constituencies had criminal records—crimes included murder, attempted murder, and criminal intimidation.[16] Corruption in the body politic also includes the mundane (but necessary) act of bribing clerks at government offices to see the correct person within a bureaucracy.

India's Economy

While IT has been the most visible industry success story for India, it is far from being the whole economic story. Gartner figures show that employment in India's ICT sector passed the one million mark in 2005, or .2 percent of the workforce. And IT's contribution to gross domestic product, while undeniably important, was only 4.7 percent of the total.[17]

India has paid a price for the slow pace of reform and a high degree of business uncertainty. Despite high levels of enthusiasm from offshore investors, the actual figures for foreign direct investment into India reflect the barriers, both perceived and actual, that remain. Annual foreign direct investment into India was $5.5 billion in 2004–2005,[18] a far cry from the $153 billion in contracted foreign direct investment enjoyed by China over the same period.

Despite these issues, the opening of India's economy is gathering speed. The Reserve Bank of India estimates that import duties have fallen from 50 percent of the value of imports in 1989–1990 to below 10 percent in 2003–2004. Over the same period, the value of imports has increased from below 9 percent of India's GDP to above 13 percent.[19] Easing of foreign investment restrictions is continuing. In January 2005 the cap on foreign direct investment in telecommunications was lifted to 74 percent.

Infrastructure

India's 1947 population of 340 million has grown threefold over sixty years to approximately 1.1 billion. This single statistic shows why some of India's problems in providing even the most basic of amenities for its population—such as running water, sanitation, and health services—remain seemingly intractable.

The per capita gross national income is $620, less than half that of China. An estimated 35 percent of Indians still live below the official poverty line. The maternal mortality rate of five hundred forty per one hundred thousand births remains one of the world's highest.[20] And in a statistic that directly refutes any idea that the booming IT industry has brought widespread prosperity to India, an estimated 60 percent of children under the age of five suffer from malnutrition.[21]

These problems with the provision of even the most basic human services naturally affect business interests across India. Energy demand has outstripped supply in many areas; some areas of India are regularly affected by drought; and antiquated airport infrastructure and control systems make some areas inaccessible by air to international visitors (and they remain difficult to access by air domestically). Delivery lead times are among the worst in the world. Many Indian cities have almost no suitable commercial premises for the demands of a modern business—companies must build their premises from scratch. A walk in almost any Indian city is an eye opener for foreign visitors unfamiliar with the country. A few blocks from the Oberoi Hotel in the center of Mumbai, Indian women can be seen carrying water drawn from public taps for their personal use.

Frustration about this lack of infrastructure was summed up by Nandan Nilekani, the chief executive of Indian outsourcer Infosys, writing about a business visit to China.[22] "In the airport lounge, I log on to the Net to see what is happening back home. 'Highway project referred to Supreme Court' . . . 'Bangalore traffic stopped for hours due to flooding' . . . 'IT companies' land should be taken away for the poor, says an ex-minister.'" Returning to Bangalore, he sees "the lonely girders of a half-built flyover, overdue by years . . . So I close my eyes and console myself that we have built a mature, functioning democracy. Surely, building an eight-lane avenue with bicycle lanes shouldn't be more difficult?"

None of the above should be read as selling India short on its many achievements, nor on its potential. Rapid improvements have occurred within India on many fronts. The average life expectancy for an Indian has increased from forty-four years in 1960 to sixty-two years in 2003. There is also government recognition of the serious infrastructure deficits. The Indian Government planned to spend $6.25 billion in 2006 in the first year of a fifteen-year project widening and paving forty thousand miles of road throughout the country.[23]

Gartner estimates that India currently receives about 80 percent of the world's spending on offshore IT outsourcing. The leading Indian companies are in a strong position to maintain this lead.[24] Spending on Indian IT services grew by an estimated 35 percent in 2005 and spending on Indian business process outsourcers grew by an estimated 45 percent in 2005 to total spending of $22.6 billion.[25] The domestic market was on the order of $36 billion for 2005, growing at a rate of 25 percent annually in the same period.

The following two chapters explore how India can continue these phenomenal growth rates in IT and related industries.

CHAPTER FIVE

India's IT Landscape Today

U NTIL RECENTLY, the Indian IT industry has been the story of the widely differing fortunes of two cousins—the export cousin and the domestic cousin. The former has been fabulously successful and richly applauded throughout the nation. The latter has been regarded as backward and hardly worth bothering about.

Much of this perception is due to the relative successes enjoyed by the export and domestic sectors of the industry. India's total exports of IT services—dominated by domestic companies, not foreign-controlled subsidiaries—were worth $21 billion in 2005.[1] In comparison, India's domestic market for IT services was worth an estimated $2.7 billion in 2005. This figure is minuscule compared to 2005 IT services spending in other countries in the region, such as Japan ($83 billion) Australia ($12.1 billion), and even China ($4.5 billion).[2]

The intensive activity supporting an export-focused industry has distorting effects across India's economy: it changes the focus of local IT firms; it influences government policy settings, such as incentives and the establishment of software technology parks; and it hampers the ability of nonexporting local employers to find and retain quality staff.

Perceptions about the successes of the rich cousin are, in some ways, mistaken. The rapid rise of the IT services and business process outsourcing (BPO) industry has been more recent and its successes more fragile than are widely supposed. And the potential of the poor cousin, while often neglected, is now being recognized both domestically and internationally.

While the export industry grew at the very impressive rate of 35 percent in 2005, the domestic IT market is forecast to grow at an impressive 25.2 percent a year up to 2009. This is the highest growth rate in the world forecast by Gartner. This compares quite favorably within the Asia Pacific region (7.9 percent), above China's projected growth rate over the same period (6.5 percent) and well above the rate forecast for established markets such as the United States (3.7 percent), Western Europe (3.1 percent), and Japan (3.2 percent). Taking into account all IT spending (including telecoms, hardware, and software), India's domestic market was worth a respectable $35.5 billion in 2005, which is predicted to grow to $84.8 billion in 2009.[3] In our view, India's domestic IT market has become an attractive destination in its own right, with expanding opportunities for foreign and domestic companies.

Export

The export side of the Indian IT industry got its big break in the early 1990s, when U.S. companies began hiring huge numbers of skilled systems analysts and computer programmers. Exporting employees from India directly to a client location was known as "body shopping." The Indian analyst or programmer was on the payroll of, say, a Tata Consultancy Services (TCS), an Infosys Technologies, or a Wipro Technologies, and these companies were delivering on a contract with a U.S. firm. Ninety percent of the revenue of these IT service firms in India came from shipping people to the United States to work onsite at the clients' locations.

Demand for Indian companies' staff in the United States was driven to frenzied levels by three factors: concern about the millennium bug, the dot-com boom, and a corporate craze for enterprise resource planning software. By 1999 Indians were by far the largest single external source (14 percent) of all foreign-born science and engineering graduates.[4] In a more prosaic way, Silicon Valley signaled this rising tide of Indian immigration when Microsoft established a campus cafeteria catered for not just Indians, but for the varied tastes of Indians hailing from the states of West Bengal, Gujarat, and Kerala.

It is only within the past five or six years that India's IT industry was transformed from a source of labor for hire to the formidable leader in IT services it is today. The fizzle of the Y2K, or millennium, bug, the dot-com bust, and enterprise resource planning disillusionment all contributed to a massive repatriation of Indian talent from the United States. A new term, "H1-B refugee," became the sobriquet for returning workers. Yet it soon acquired a halo effect and became a marketable badge of honor: these H-1B refugees were an important ingredient in the resurgent IT services industry in India. This talent—with continuing relationships at U.S. firms and strong credibility—gave Indian companies an important foot in the door. Supported by high-speed, high-bandwidth telecom connectivity, Indian companies could continue to offer diverse world-class IT services to customers in the United States and, increasingly, the United Kingdom. These were the building blocks for today's IT industry in India.[5]

The international success is clear. India has captured approximately two-thirds of the world's offshore services business, including offshore IT and the fast-growing BPO market. Indian companies that are now seen as viable competitors with much larger U.S. outsourcing firms, such as EDS and IBM, include TCS, Wipro, Infosys, Cognizant Technologies, Satyam Computer Services, and HCL Technologies. Some of the larger Indian companies now span the globe. TCS, for one, aspires to be a top ten IT service provider by 2010. It has offices in thirty-four countries and counts six of the *Fortune* top ten companies among its customers. India's strength in IT is built predominantly on contracts with U.S. multinational companies and, to a lesser but increasing extent, U.K.-based companies. Until recently, Indian IT services firms had limited success in emerging markets in Europe, Japan, and Korea.

Why have the Indian firms had more difficulty outside the United States and the United Kingdom? Initially, there was simply an abundance of U.S. and U.K. demand, and the Indian companies had their hands full keeping up. More recently, as they pursued clients in continental Europe as well as in Asia Pacific, they have been hampered by language and cultural issues in Germany, France, and Japan—the three most important markets after the United States and the United Kingdom.

Indian companies have not been able to replicate their experience in the U.S and U.K. markets in these newer markets. They have had to learn to do business in a new way. Companies in these markets are more risk-averse and conservative; they were slower to see the quality and cost-reduction potential of offshore services. However, that mindset appears to be changing, in part because use of offshore talent is perceived to have given strong competitive advantages to U.S. and U.K. competitors. Continental Europe has emerged as the fastest growing offshore market today, albeit from initially small total revenues.

Japanese companies also became more aggressive in working with Indian IT service providers in 2006, to judge from the mounting volume of inquiries Gartner receives from them. Australia is another emerging market for Indian service providers in Asia Pacific, and we expect that Korea and China soon will join the Aussies.

What does this growth in other markets portend for U.S. and U.K. clients of the Indian IT service firms? First, the Indian IT service firms are adjusting their investment priorities to accommodate the new growth, which could reduce or slow future capabilities in the United States and the United Kingdom. Second, there will be stronger competition for the offshore providers' best talents and other resources among their blue-chip client enterprises across three continents. The offshore providers' trade-offs on urgent resource allocations, for example, will need to be made among companies like GE (based in the United States), Philips (based in the Netherlands), Sony (with headquarters in Japan), and possibly Samsung (Korea) or Haier (China). This means that CIOs of clients in the United States and the United Kingdom, long treated as kings of the offshore mountain, should prepare to negotiate effectively with an eye toward attracting and retaining essential high-quality resources on their projects. The Indian IT service firms also need to develop the capability to take advantage of future opportunities for IT services in China—an effort already underway and described in chapter 7.

The Domestic Market

The inward-focused domestic IT industry has gone through a more convulsive change, even more recently. After operating many years in a protectionist economy, India's domestic industries generally saw little reason to invest in IT or other productivity drivers. They had more than enough customer demand to satisfy their production capacity. For example, customers of Bajaj, a domestic manufacturer of scooters, motorcycles, and three-wheelers, had to wait several years to buy a vehicle. Without competition, what was the point in investing in IT to gain efficiencies? On the supply side, Indian IT companies were making as much money as they could in offshore markets, at much higher revenue and margins than the domestic industry—and all of it tax-free. This has contributed to a neglect of local Indian IT needs that exists to this day.

India's economic liberalization over the past ten years has spurred a new era of global competitors entering domestic Indian industries, from automobiles to insurance. In turn, India's stronger domestic enterprises have geared up to face this competition by increasingly turning to IT to match the high levels of efficiency, productivity, customer focus, market responsiveness, and so on that these global competitors have been pursuing for years. Indian companies in many industries, from manufacturing to financial services, are turning the tables and going global in their own expansion plans.

Again, IT-driven performance is a key element in the often superior operations Indian executives see in their competitors. This is the result of many years of effective IT investment, usage, and deployment. The Indian executives understand this and are aggressively pursuing catch-up strategies to pare down and ultimately eliminate the structural disadvantages their companies face after years of underinvestment in IT. This embrace of IT by Indian executives also was spurred by recent steps taken by Prime Minister Singh's coalition government to accelerate liberalization of the economy.

All these factors have contributed to increased interest by global companies in India's local opportunities. India's poor cousin is starting to get some attention from outside India. In fact, the majority of the largest IT services or outsourcing deals that Indian companies have signed have been awarded to global IT firms, not to the leading firms based in India. For this reason, Indian IT companies targeting only domestic customers remain small and vulnerable to acquisition compared with their counterparts focused on global corporate giants. While TCS was the largest supplier of IT services in India, with an estimated $216 million of revenue in 2004–2005, this accounted only for 12 percent of its total revenues.[6] TCS was only one of three Indian companies in the top ten, the others being GTL and Wipro Infotech.[7]

TCS's capabilities, however, were judged an also-ran to foreign competitors when India's major mobile telephone company, Bharti Tele-Ventures, went shopping for IT suppliers. In February 2004 Bharti signed a $400 million, three-year deal with Sweden's Ericsson to maintain and build its mobile telephone network. In March 2004 Bharti signed a $700 million ten-year deal with U.S.-based IBM to provide IT services. In May 2004 Bharti signed a $275 million, three-year deal with Finland's Nokia to further expand and maintain its network in India. In July 2004 it signed a $50 million deal with Germany's Siemens for further expansion and maintenance.[8] And in August 2005 Bharti signed another deal with Nokia, this time for $125 million, to expand its network again, deeper into India's rural areas. These moves to completely outsource its network while focusing on rapidly growing customer numbers have won Bharti international attention. It added 3.65 million customers for a total subscriber base of nearly 25 million in the second quarter of 2006, with sales rising 53 percent, to $838 million.[9]

While Bharti's outsourcing model is widely regarded as leading edge, the absence of Indian suppliers on this roll call of deals can be interpreted in three ways. First, Indian companies were asleep when international companies grew successful businesses in India. Second, Indian companies may not have been able to seize the opportunities—particularly in relation to the cutting-edge domain expertise on a global scale that companies like Bharti were seeking—even if they wanted to. Finally, the poor cousin may not be so poor after all and is finally rewarding those companies that have actively courted it.

What can CIOs of global companies learn from Bharti's strategy? First, it addresses a key problem that many subsidiaries of global companies are facing: staffing their local IT departments in India. This is a new challenge. Staff scarcity is reflected in staff turnover generally, with foreign companies also vulnerable to the perceived prestige of employment with a major Indian outsourcer. There is a distinct food chain of employment within India, with large Indian offshore providers at the top and government employment at the bottom. Everyone else, ranging from global service providers and global software vendors to captive centers and large Indian enterprises and so on, fall in the middle. Then too, as in most countries, some geographic locations are more appealing to employees than others. Thus location increasingly is a factor in rates of employee retention.

The Bharti case shows that the domestic Indian IT industry is attracting greater interest from Indian IT employees for potential job opportunities. Also, IT service providers are reallocating some resources to the domestic Indian IT industry and away from export activity. To compete, global companies must first move up the *employment* food chain and the *service-provider* food chain to secure support for their local operations, many of which are being expanded. Second, the captive centers of these global companies—typically IT or BPO offices set up to provide global support to the parent company—also must move up the employment food chain. The global parent companies must be able to acquire and retain high-quality resources for these captive centers.

This trend is also significant for global IT providers. The Indian domestic market is the fastest growing in the world and offers many opportunities for IT vendors beyond global service providers—such as IBM,

Accenture, or EDS—that are setting up offshore centers in India. Vendors across all realms of information and communications technology (ICT)—including software, hardware, networking and telecom, storage, and so on—will see increasing opportunities in the Indian domestic market. Early entrants will be able to establish more committed relationships that will form significant barriers to entry for later competitors.

Demand Side: Export and Domestic

The stark differences between India's export and domestic IT are mirrored in their widely divergent customer bases. On the one hand, large multinational and national corporations are aiming for cost savings from increasingly complex IT outsourcing projects. On the other hand, a large, small to medium business base within India is, in some cases, only just now considering IT investments. As these companies start investing in IT, we believe in fact there are reasons to be optimistic about the potential of a wide range of would-be IT customers within India. Gartner's forecast of 25.2 percent compound growth over four years will result in total ICT spending in the domestic market of $84.6 billion in 2009.

A picture of some of India's peculiarities as a market can be seen by comparing spending in sectors in India with comparable spending in a mature market, such as the United States. In India, estimated spending in 2004 was dominated by telecom (80 percent), followed by hardware (11 percent), IT services (7 percent), and software (2 percent). This split is expected to remain roughly the same over the next four-year period. In the United States, estimated spending in 2005 was also dominated by telecom, but to a much lesser degree, at 48 percent. In contrast to India, a much greater proportion of spending in the United States went to IT services (30 percent), hardware (15 percent), and software (7 percent).

The skew in spending toward telecommunications is largely explained by the relatively nascent stage of development of the industry in India, with India likely to be playing a decades-long game of catch-up.

Opportunities in Mobile Telecoms

Indian businesses are increasing their investments in wireless technologies, led by mobile messaging and e-mail applications, but they are proceeding cautiously. Problems with unreliable or unavailable services persist in several cities in India.[10]

Apart from basic cellular voice services, business wireless products are fairly limited, and the market is underdeveloped. This presents an opportunity for global mobile telecommunications companies because the markets offer rapid growth and potentially high volume. Then too the Indian government recently opened the domestic mobile industry to greater foreign investment. It lifted the ceiling on foreign direct investment in the telecommunications industry to 74 percent in January 2005, from 49 percent.

Many Indian telecoms are expanding to provincial areas and can benefit quickly from foreign investment. Robust and reliable service in these provincial areas is a priority. These companies will look for fairly simple applications that can be scaled up or integrated with existing applications as they expand into even more rural areas.

Domestic businesses will continue to favor mainstream applications based on familiar technology platforms like SMS (short messaging service). SMS text messages, which may be up to one hundred sixty characters in length, are less expensive than voice calls or Internet access, and can be sent to mobile phones from computers, other phones, or the Internet.

Text messaging is more popular in India, other parts of Asia, and Europe than in the United States. The market in India is expected to grow rapidly as more global companies set up new offices or expand existing operations. Moreover, these enterprises are likely to spend actively for other wireless technologies, such as e-mail and sales force automation, that are well established in their bigger markets.

Integrated telecom providers will have the advantage in marketing and selling these products and services. They can bundle mobile services with corporate data, broadband access, and other services to become a preferred carrier. Another advantage for global players in mobile telecoms is that increasing investments and operations in India should make it easier to partner with India's world-class companies in software development to create advanced products and services for global markets.

A survey in early 2006 of nearly one hundred fifty technology leaders, typically CIOs or IT managers, in government and several industrial sectors showed that more than 30 percent of Indian companies with revenues of more than $1 billion spent more than $500,000 a year on wireless mobile equipment and services. Organizations with more than five thousand employees, or 21 percent of respondents, spent more than $100,000.

The relatively low spending on IT services can be explained by the lack of attention to the domestic industry combined with low wage rates of Indian staff. Nevertheless, Gartner forecasts strong annual growth in all areas through 2009, including telecom (20 percent a year), IT services (17 percent), software (16 percent), and hardware (14 percent). This demand will come predominantly from telecom companies, followed by financial services companies. Sharing third place more or less will be the government, manufacturing, and services companies.

Large corporations operating in India will provide another area of appealing growth for all IT companies. In February 2004, for instance, the Bank of India signed a ten-year deal with Hewlett-Packard (HP) to outsource its IT needs for $150 million. Yet outside these "big-bang" contracts, small to medium-sized businesses present good opportunities for IT vendors. This outlook presumes that business models can be developed around low-cost delivery of both hardware and services. There are also growing signs of rising government spending on IT projects. For example, the Ministry of Company Affairs is spending an estimated $75 million digitizing the records from its Registrar of Companies. TCS and one of its local subsidiaries, CMC Limited, won the contract.

In light of several positive indicators, including strong economic growth, an easing regulatory environment, proactive government policies, and rapidly falling prices for international telecommunications (80 percent in the past three years, and still falling), there are good grounds for seeing India as a highly prospective market. Many international vendors have secured substantial footholds in the market already. IBM was second to TCS in IT services in 2004–2005, with an estimated $102 million in revenues. HP was fifth with $72 million and Covansys was sixth with $48 million.[11] The low-cost model offered by India is underpinned by relatively lower wages, with average programmer salaries remaining near $10,000 annually, compared with about $65,000 in the United States.[12]

Challenges

Of course there are a host of sobering challenges in the domestic market that must be considered by both entrants and outsourcers. Labor union opposition to any kind of automation, though substantially muted now, persists. Recourse to the law in cases of service disputes is seen as time-consuming and very possibly ineffective. And there is an inherent reluctance within Indian businesses to outsource vital IT processes, a bias for self-sufficiency probably rooted in India's strongly socialist heritage that shaped its domestic and foreign policies and experience for decades after independence. During this period, there simply was no one else to deliver services, and companies had to rely on internal resources. But the major challenges for foreign IT companies continuing to make any headway in India remain the two identified in the previous chapter: infrastructure and available talent.

The Indian IT services export industry can earn such extraordinary profits in world markets relative to the domestic industry that skilled IT labor and IT services are actually in short supply. For example, university graduates will leave domestic company IT departments after seven to twelve months of training because they can substantially boost their salaries by going with an IT services firm selling offshore services. Software developers have no incentive to create packaged applications for the domestic market when more money can be earned in offshore application development. IT service providers limit or refuse domestic business because greater margins can be earned from global clients.[13]

In Gartner's study of suitable destinations in India for foreign companies, both Bangalore and New Delhi were judged to have declining abilities to retain talent, while Mumbai was neutral. And cost of living—indicating pressure on wages—was seen to be increasing in all three cities.[14] Add to this the lower levels of English capability in some of the emerging cities discussed earlier, and we see a difficult environment continuing for hiring and retaining skilled staff. Concerns about retention and recruitment go a long way toward explaining why India's leading IT services firms recently made their first significant investments in China (see chapter 7): access to the highly motivated and lower-cost engineering graduates being turned out in increasing numbers by China's well-funded, elite universities.

Infrastructure issues will also plague both domestic and foreign companies for many years. The much vaunted government initiative of founding software technology parks simply supports islands of infrastructure that cannot possibly address the infrastructure problems beyond their gates. According to International Telecommunication Union estimates, there were only 71 phones—fixed and mobile—for every 1,000 residents in 2003.[15] This compares poorly with China (424) and the United States (1,164).

But the deficit goes beyond poor performance in energy, transportation, and telecommunications infrastructure, which, despite recent investments, remain problematic. Less than 1 percent of the target audience has broadband connection, a staggering deficit that undermines adoption of IT services of all kinds in all areas.[16] And, in a country of 1.1 billion people, India accounted for only about 4.4 million computers shipped in 2005—yet another measure of very limited infrastructure for IT. To be sure, the numbers of Indian digerati are accelerating rapidly. In 2000 an estimated 4.5 million personal computers were operating in the whole country.[17] Yet the wired nation of India still compares poorly with neighboring China, where 17.2 million computers were shipped in 2005.[18]

Most of India's personal computers are operated by their owners in urban areas. And most IT employees among them would be able to telecommute if their companies allowed it. But Indian customs laws require that employees of the Indian IT offshore service firms must perform their work at a "bonded" premise of the employer or the IT service firms. This rules out telecommuting among one of India's most qualified employee group.

The low telecommuting numbers notwithstanding, the rapid growth of Internet connectivity in India, including broadband services (again primarily concentrated in the urban areas), is creating a work-from-home style of living that embraces a new variation (for India) called "work-from-hometown." Sun Microsystems India has been an early adopter of this new trend for India's IT industry. Sun not only allows employees to work from home as required, it also allows key employees to work from home and not relocate to cities where Sun offices are located. If it catches on, this trend could have huge implications for India's IT employers in their strategies to compete in global markets. If job location dims as an employment factor in India, the market for India's world-class IT talent could open up impressively. IT employers—global and domestic—will be able to recruit and bid more aggressively for brainpower with less regard for relocation costs, which may be unnecessary.

These issues have effects on India's domestic and international aspirations. Gartner recently predicted that India's dominant global market share of approximately 70 percent in offshore outsourcing would fall over time. The good news for India, though, is that global demand for offshore services, both in ITO as well as BPO, is rising so fast that revenue growth for India-based companies still should increase rapidly.[19] What could conspire against this optimistic forecast? The usual suspects in India: inadequate human resources and poor infrastructure. High staff turnover; lack of managerial talent; poor power, water, and transportation infrastructure; inconsistent telecommunications policies; saturation of stretched infrastructure in major cities—indeed, as discussed in the next chapter, India's desire and will to catch up to the world's modern economies with regard to human resources and infrastructure will largely determine what kind of IT juggernaut—if any at all—India will become by the middle of this century.

Talent and the "Big Picture"

A perceived lack of managerial talent is a pressing issue for Indian companies facing an increasingly hostile competitive environment. Gartner estimates there are now fifty separate countries that, collectively, are threatening India's dominance in the supply of offshore IT services. Moreover, there are in excess of two hundred global service providers with operations in India. Many of them, based in foreign countries, hope to emulate Indian companies' offshore performances or prospect for work within India's borders. Indeed, we have been advising clients in China's emerging IT services sector to look for client opportunities there.

India has also been notably absent in the development of a local IT hardware industry, in stark contrast to China. This is a result of the Indian government's protectionist policies in the industry since the early 1970s that barred foreign investment inflows. In fact, a single event contributed greatly to India's long-standing IT doldrums—the expulsion of IBM in the early 1970s, along with other global icons, such as Coca-Cola, by a rabidly socialist government that feared monopolistic behavior by these global giants. The ban continued into the early 1980s, when a return of the Congress government reversed some of these blatant protectionist policies. With IBM a nonfactor in India during this period, a number of indigenous IT companies sprang up. The first was Computer Maintenance Corporation (CMC Limited), a government entity whose lone purpose was maintaining IBM computers that were installed prior to IBM's departure. Would the evolution of India's IT industry have been more rapid and advanced if IBM had remained the driving force during those crucial ten years? Probably.

In contrast, foreign direct investment was embraced increasingly by the Beijing government in the 1980s and 1990s. The foreign money flow has underpinned China's rapid rise to its factory-of-the-world status. Standing on the sidelines, India's manufacturing capabilities have lagged far behind the world's standards.

Old India hands also remember, with some frustration, the brief moment late in 2001 when Azim Premji, the chief executive of Wipro, became the second richest man due to soaring stock prices on the

Mumbai Stock Exchange. Premji did not seize the moment with a major, stock-based acquisition for Wipro. Consequently, Wipro did not take its place on the world stage.

This lack of management daring and the poor perception of India's educational system raise questions inside and outside India about whether its corporations have the firepower to become truly global. Premji himself has been active on the education front, establishing the Azim Premji Foundation and aiming to foster universal education at primary schools. "Almost every economist, industry expert, business person, and management guru is expressing that by 2020, India can be among the top two superpowers in the world in terms of contribution to world GDP," he said in 2004. "By 2020 we can also become the largest talent pool. This dream will not materialize if we do not ensure education for all children."[20]

Tomorrow

Many Indian companies are not letting the grass grow under their feet. Three works-in-progress serve to demonstrate the opportunities for foreign companies, for the domestic industry, and for the export industry. U.S.-based Intel—which already employs three thousand Indians at its Bangalore R&D center—has invested $250 million in partnership with local manufacturer Xenitis Infotech to manufacture low-cost computers priced at $250—the cheapest machine for sale with an Intel chip. The target market is regional and rural areas within India.[21] On the domestic side, Bharti Tele-Ventures is growing in innovative, unexpected ways. Bharti and IBM are establishing an IT services business that seeks business from domestic customers. On the export side, as mentioned, all major Indian IT outsourcers have established beachhead offices in China, with a view to leveraging their IT services skills, not just in China but also in the more insular Korean and Japanese markets.[22]

These three examples show Indian companies can be innovative (Bharti), build capacity in areas not generally seen as a strength (Xenitis's alliance with Intel), and be aggressive in expanding beyond a predominant U.S. focus into Asian markets generally. Indeed, these kinds of talents have put Indian companies on the threshold of what we believe could develop into one of the great economic success stories of the pan-Asian region: the great global potential of India and China together, combining the world's IT services powerhouse with the world's factory.

Anyone doubting India's capacity to play its part need only consider the source of its IT industry. In 1995–1996 India's exports of IT services were worth about $1 million.[23] In 2004 they were worth $13 billion. In 2000 India's share of BPO was worth $148 million.[24] In 2004 it was worth $3.5 billion. Any student of business knows what those kinds of growth rates mean: disruptive, challenging forces that can unseat rivals and destroy business plans.

CHAPTER

Charting the Course
for India to 2012

WITH ITS CHALLENGING LOGISTICS, stifling bureaucracy, official corruption, and leftist political influences,
can India still be worth the effort? We hear this question often from
CIOs, business strategists, and decision makers who doubt whether the
benefits of an Indian connection can truly outweigh obvious risks and
discomforts. The vast majority of the global *Fortune* 1,000 companies
have agreed that India *is* worth the effort. And, in the main, they go to India to buy what India does better than any country in the world: IT services and, increasingly, business process outsourcing (BPO).

Gartner's analysis of the world's thirty leading IT services firms in
January 2006 shows that seven of the top ten providers of high-quality,
low-cost software programming and call-center operations were India-
based companies. They included the four global leaders as measured by
completeness of vision and ability to execute in applications services—
Tata Consultancy Services (TCS), Infosys Technologies, Wipro Technologies, and Cognizant Technologies. The next two, Accenture and
IBM, had major IT services operations in India.[1]

Yes, we think India is worth the effort when the problems you are attacking and opportunities you are chasing match what India can provide. We estimate that the largest IT services providers will add between fifteen thousand and thirty thousand employees *annually,* on average, for the next several years in anticipation of continued rapid growth in global demand. This chapter explains the key uncertainties that global strategists and decision makers face in deciding how and whether to engage with India's ICT industry and presents our vision of the three most plausible scenario paths this industry is likely to take in the next five years.

This chapter focuses on critical uncertainties in India as the background for the anticipated milestones and signposts leading to the possible scenarios for that country. The reasons for this approach are directly tied to the considerable, often confounding difficulties business strategists confront in forecasting economic policy in the world's largest democracy. Those analyzing potential scenarios for the Indian IT market are well advised to consider shifting political alliances and implications for the IT industry's policy agenda.

We place a similar emphasis on government policy in our China analysis. In truth, however, the political dynamics in India are far more daunting. As noted, majority consensus is difficult to achieve among India's federal and state lawmakers. Once achieved, majority consensus is more difficult to sustain and implement. Moreover, government elections and budget processes that can weaken, reverse, or accelerate existing policy seem never to end. Business leaders are left to place long-term bets with short-term visibility into policy—a complaint often heard in Washington, D.C., London, Frankfurt, and other capitals of capitalist democracies.

IT leaders and business decision makers must understand how sudden power shifts on major political debates in India can affect strategy and operations. The analysis should not be deflected to junior staffers or ignored outright. An important part of your role may well be to oversee contingency plans that prepare your enterprise to adapt quickly when the unexpected occurs. These contingency plans must reflect political reality—and political possibility.

India is easily the bigger challenge for business because government is still finding its way, haltingly at times, into a global capitalist system after shedding decades of socialist doctrine in the early 1990s. In China, by contrast, the Chinese Communist Party acts as a selective filter of capitalist policy options it has experimented with for nearly thirty years. Once decisions are made, party leaders drive a top-down agenda supported by huge budgets and a general cultural adherence to official authority.

Moreover, India's role in the supply-demand economy of global technology is much more recent than China. The Y2K buildup and dot-com boom that ignited demand for India's low-cost software programmers occurred less than ten years ago. The rise of India's now predominant IT offshore outsourcing firms and call centers soon followed. Add to this a surge in mobile telecommunications now underway, potential policy reforms on the dockets in New Delhi and several state capitals, and accelerating in-country activities by major global IT companies, including Nokia, IBM, Microsoft, Dell, and Intel. There is little doubt that the immediate future of the ICT industry in India harbors many latent opportunities and threats for CIOs and their colleagues.

Critical Uncertainty One: Availability of Qualified Resources

Qualified resources is our term for a well-trained, creative, and innovative workforce. Considering India's huge population, concern about a shortage of people might seem counterintuitive, but we emphasize the word "qualified"—meaning appropriately trained for a specific job. We are talking about the right mix of talented people with the collective skill sets to match the full range of workplace opportunities and challenges at hand.

The vertical axis in figure 6-1 corresponds to the range of availability and qualifications for India's IT workforce. The low end of the spectrum, labeled "purely technical" is not far from the reality in India today. It suggests a workforce with capabilities that are well suited for formulaic, high-volume, repetitive tasks, like writing software codes in Web-based languages such as Microsoft's .Net or Sun Microsystem's Java, trouble-shooting IT system breakdowns, processing tax forms, evaluating medical X-rays, or following scripted responses at outsourced call centers. There is an abundance of this talent in India.

At the top of the scale, we have in mind brilliant, creative, and innovative analysts and thinkers. That is part of it. Another part is a sophistication in behavioral and communications skills associated with effective leaders, often called emotional intelligence. These so-called soft skills are imperative for successful collaboration across cultures and boundaries in the global IT industry. In India they are still in short supply, even among India's leading IT services firms.

These gaps create real and costly setbacks. The CIO of a large U.S.-based organization, a client of one of India's top IT services providers, gave us this first-hand account. After a deadline was missed, an Indian project team spent three hours with the client project manager in the

FIGURE 6-1

India's ICT landscape in 2012

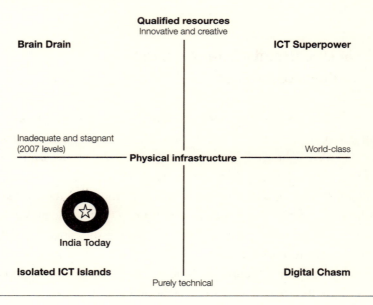

United States reviewing options to get back on track. The client suggested a series of actions in a "can't miss" process that everyone agreed would get the project finished within a month after the original target. The Indian team implemented the steps and the new deadline was met. Weeks later, one of the Indian programmers casually told a member of the U.S. client team that a different approach could have delivered the same results within just two weeks, not one month. The Indian team did not bring it up during the long meeting because, he said, "Your manager told us what you wanted us to do. We did not want to create any waves in such a tense situation."

That logic—better go along to get along—is a fool's comfort for the Indian service providers. If the Indian firms cannot get their better ideas onto the table at the right time and in the right place, clients in developed economies will either develop better ideas themselves or contract with service firms in other countries and cultures that can. When our CIO friend heard from his team what happened with the Indian firm, he stiffened procedures to require his project managers to formally seek options and recommendations from the Indian teams. "We learned the hard way to put more trust in their abilities," he said. "We ask the providers for their proposals before we put forward our own."

This is good news in one sense for Indian service providers: U.S. clients recognize that they should put greater trust in the Indians. But there was more news coming from this CIO. He now would expect more initiative from account managers representing Indian offshore service firms. "We now insist that the account manager from the IT services provider be present at these schedule-recovery meetings," he told us. "Moreover, the services provider must screen this manager in advance to have the self-confidence and the authority to raise an objection and tell us if we're wrong or there is a better way."

"A lot of our work requires very high collaboration skills and blue-sky thinking with our IT service partners," the CIO continued. "They have to be ready to debate as equals with everyone on my team. Frankly, I am not sure any Indian service provider can do this. We could do blue-sky analysis in-house in the U.S., but increasingly I prefer the idea of establishing my own captive center in India." The CIO's message is that

India has plenty of talent capable of collaborating on high-level problems and opportunities. That talent can be trained to his standards in India if his team controls the process. At this point, though, he lacks confidence in India's IT services providers or India's educational system to develop this talent on its own.

A handful of U.S.-based global IT companies are now establishing captive centers in research and development. Intel, for one, created its Centrino Duo mobile platform chip primarily at its India Development Center. About five hundred employees there participated in an eighteen-month, design-to-market project that invented smaller form factors, more battery life, and less power consumption better suited for mobile entertainment. Intel praised the results in early 2006 as "a path breaking effort by Intel India."[2] Overall, Intel India employs 3,000 people near Bangalore, including twenty-seven hundred engineers, scientists, and other technology staff. The company invested $700 million there in the previous decade, with plans to invest another $1 billion in its India R&D operations by 2011.[3]

Symantec, a global leader in software security services, gave a green light in 2005 for Symantec India in Pune to pursue new product road maps independently. It was a first for any Symantec R&D lab outside the United States. The center employs about eleven hundred people, including about 20 percent of Symantec's R&D staff worldwide. Symantec, based in Cupertino, California, handed regional product management duties to the Pune center just two months after Symantec's 2005 acquisition of Veritas Software. Veritas was an early mover in India, operating the Pune development center since 1992. Symantec's quick embrace underscored Veritas's success in assembling world-class R&D talent in India.[4]

"Opportunities for new products managed within India are rising as the Indian market and much of the Asia Pacific region elsewhere grow larger and more sophisticated," said Sharad Sharma, Symantec's vice president for product operations and general manager for India. "We will be focused on global markets, but with customer access and insight coming from regional markets," he said.[5]

India also has homegrown examples of IT innovation. One of the better known is Pentamedia Graphics, of Chennai. Pentamedia was the first major movie production house to use the technique of motion capture in a full-length, animated 3D film when it created *Sinbad: Beyond the Veils of the Mists*. The movie was completed in just eighteen months at a cost of $14 million—far less than the $40 million it would have cost to produce the film anywhere else in the world. A commercial success as well as a technology breakthrough, the film has sparked India's emergence as a new destination for the international animation and special effects industry.[6]

Despite these recent successes and the much documented superiority of India's IT services firms in offshore services and business process outsourcing, a talent shortage is looming for India's ICT industry. India's existing resource pool is exactly suited for the quality of work that is generating $26 billion in annual revenues *now* for India's IT offshore service companies. The vast majority of Indian ICT employees today learn the *what*—the programming skills required to do their jobs—and they learn the *how*—the precise process steps to excel in highly repeatable and predictable tasks.

But Filipinos can learn the what and the how too. So can the Russians, the Chinese, the Hungarians, and the Mexicans. And they are. Gartner's most recent tally identified fifty-four countries competing for the kind of offshore services work pioneered by India. Labor cost arbitrage, in the buzzwords of globalization—the basic value proposition is to match or exceed India's skills at lower cost. Some countries already are succeeding in taking a piece of this pie from India: others will follow. Moreover, as our CIO friend notes, many clients of India's offshore providers are exploring how to establish sophisticated captive centers in the backyards of these providers.

Breaking with the past, these centers exemplify a race-to-the-top urgency that is pulsing across the global IT industry. They will focus on specific, high-margin opportunities in the global market by leveraging the creativity of their most brilliant scientists and technologists wherever they can assemble them. This constraint in top-notch talent is acknowledged even among the most enthusiastic global IT companies expanding in India. Dell, for instance, is bullish on India in part because it sees huge growth in PC demand in India, with its current shipments of five million PCs expected to double by 2010. Dell also sees India as one of the world's most attractive places to harvest talent for transaction processing, R&D, and IT operations, as well as for creating a manufacturing base.

The biggest uncertainty for Dell in planning and implementing strategies in India, as well as other locations outside the United States, "is the talent supply, particularly in middle management," Rohit Malhotra, managing director of Dell's Indian operations, said in a *McKinsey Quarterly* interview. "The reason we have three [call] centers in India, and not six isn't that we don't have the demand; it's because we are talent-constrained. It takes time to get the right people to come in and then teach them the Dell culture to make sure they can succeed in this environment . . . [W]e're starting from a very low base, but in three to five years' time, recruitment and training will be much easier."[7]

If the talent turns out to be too thin in India, decision factors for locating sophisticated captive centers will be revisited, and these centers could go elsewhere—perhaps to China or Russia. This would be a blow to the long-term potential of India's ICT industry. The IT services firms themselves could face a dramatic slowdown in offshore demand if they are unable to put more thinkers on client project teams, and that would be another strike against India's ICT industry. The biggest threat to India's "brute force" model of providing offshore IT services featuring legions of heads-down doers is technology itself; namely, automation. This trend of substituting capital for labor has already played out in systems management and operations domain, with staffing levels dramatically reduced by technology advances. There is no reason to believe the same trend will not cut into staffing levels for programming and call-center services.

Critical Uncertainty Two: Infrastructure

The second critical uncertainty that will determine India's future in global ICT is the country's infrastructure—roads, highways, bridges, seaports, subways, buses and trains, airports and airlines, electric power and water utilities, telecommunications systems, and so on. In figure 6-1, the far-left end of the horizontal axis represents very inadequate and stagnant levels of India's physical infrastructure.

Those within India's fast-rising IT community sadly ponder what could have been—and what yet could be—if India's infrastructure were the equal of any developed economy in the world. In its most recent report on global competitiveness, the World Economic Forum confirmed what millions of Indians and foreign business travelers to India know too well: "an inadequate supply of infrastructure" is by far the largest impediment to doing business in India.[8] Indian executives themselves rank poor infrastructure as their biggest major concern, ahead of lack of access to capital, inadequate legal protection, excessive regulation and vulnerability to rising energy prices.[9]

The problem of India's infrastructure is clearly an important issue for the IT industry. Shipments cannot be guaranteed to arrive on time. Rail networks are inadequate. Electric power and other energy supplies are erratic. Telecommunications networks are unreliable. Roads are inferior. One Chinese IT services firm we know believes that India's abysmal infrastructure provides a contrast so shocking compared with China's modern cities and highways that the Chinese firm happily pays for prospective clients to visit India and see conditions there firsthand. More often than not, the Chinese executives tell us, a decision in their favor is guaranteed before final negotiations are completed back in China.

The far right end of the horizontal axis in the figure represents what would in effect be a realization of the vision of the IT community: a world-class infrastructure to rival the best systems in the world's developed economies. To create a world-class infrastructure, India requires a high level of investment through government spending and increased reliance on foreign direct investment (FDI).

Infrastructure breakdowns, logjams, and persistent crowding certainly hamper business activity in India's major IT cities. One morning in 2006, Partha was on his way to participate in a panel discussion on biotechnology that an important global client had organized on its campus on the southern outskirts of Bangalore. He had less than ten miles to travel from his hotel but, anticipating the notorious traffic jams along Bangalore's lone main road to Electronic City, he had blocked out an hour and a half for the trip in his rental car. He nearly missed the start of his panel. Southbound traffic, backed up for miles, had been forced into one lane. When he finally inched his way to where he could see the cause of the roadblock, Partha could only laugh. A large elephant was lumbering slowly along in the right lane with his caretaker. Nearby, a partially built highway overpass was still under construction, four years after the first concrete had been poured. This infamous "flyover," with a completion date unfathomable by jaded commuters (see Nandan Nilekani's frustrated comment in chapter 4), might have helped matters that day. But in the eyes of hundreds of thousands in the global IT community who have seen it, the flyover's sole purpose is to stand as a dispiriting icon of India's long-running ineptitude with infrastructure.

Life in India's major cities is challenging for IT professionals both on and off the job. A normal commute requires about two hours each way along crowded, polluted roads that are pockmarked with potholes. The city of Bangalore, for instance, counted more than thirty-one thousand potholes along its roads in 2005. Public buses are rarely seen. Most travelers commute by two-wheelers (motor scooters) or company-owned buses. Many midlevel managers in these companies drive their own cars, especially if they need to coordinate their schedules with workday hours in the United States and other Western economies. For them, driving to and from work over long distances is the only real option. Interruptions of electric power supplies are ubiquitous and unpredictable. They prevent children from studying at night, force residents of high-rise buildings to walk the stairs when elevator service is out, and generally complicate even the most dedicated persons' efforts to better their lives.

Global IT employers know that it can be more difficult for professionals to be productive under these conditions in India than in cities where lights typically go on when a switch is flipped and buses, trains, and subways run on time. Several employers long ago decided to take matters into their own hands. Many of India's IT services firms own and operate business campuses with their own electricity supplies, employee transport systems and, in some cases, even hotel accommodations for visitors. Infosys, for instance, is one of the largest electric power generators in the city of Bangalore.

It also has entered the hotel business. With seventy to one hundred daily visitors to its suburban campus, fifteen thousand full-time employees in Bangalore, and a dearth of affordable guest rooms available in the city, Infosys built a five hundred-room hotel complex in 2005 that quickly registered occupancy rates of more than 90 percent.[10] Customers and employees from distant locations gladly use the rooms, which offer the lavish comforts of five-star hotels.

"India is running out of capacity in many areas—airports, roads and hotels," Infosys's then chief financial officer (now director of human resources), T. V. Mohandas Pai, told the *Hindu Business Line*. "People like us depend on international business. Therefore, it is imperative that our business visitors travel easily and stay comfortably."[11] In effect, after assessing its large presence and potential exposure in Bangalore, Infosys is protecting its global headquarters investments and client relationships by vertically integrating from IT services delivery into the fringes of private travel services and public infrastructure.

An obvious second option for the global IT industry is to build a presence in other cities in India where government officials are more welcoming.[12] In India, assessing the degree of "welcoming" by government officials is often difficult because of shifting political sands. Nevertheless, we advise clients to keep an open mind. A good example is the state of West Bengal and its state capital Kolkata (Calcutta). IBM, TCS, and Wipro are among the 180 IT services firms that collectively employ 18,000 people in this northeastern city of 14 million. American International Group, the global insurer and sophisticated IT user, operates a software development center. We agree with a TCS executive, Ajoyendra Mukherjee, who concluded in 2004 that Kolkata "has all root requirements for IT: good communications, good power supply, intellectual talent, low attrition rates and, in recent years, a responsive government."[13]

And here may be the biggest surprise. State government in West Bengal is dominated by Communists, who swept nearly 70 percent of the votes in a May 2006 election. Yet these West Bengal Communists appear to have much more in common with Chinese Communists in embracing capitalist ideas dear to global IT companies than the anti-reform Communists at the center (federal level) in the Congress Party's national governing coalition in India. In a step to attract further investment in the high-growth IT sector, the West Bengal coalition government led by the Communist Party of India (Marxist) reclassified IT and related services as essential public utilities in 2006. And these Communists decided to ban labor strikes.[14] Could Marx or Lenin ever have envisioned such a day? "Globalization is inevitable and we cannot shy away from that," the Marxist Chief Minister of West Bengal, Buddhadeb Bhattacharjee, told the *India Daily*.[15]

Our analysis of potential city locations for IT operations in India includes four categories, with Bangalore, Mumbai, and New Delhi regarded as superior, first-tier cities because of their access to the best workforces, infrastructure, ease of access for international travelers, and lifestyle. Chennai, Gurgaon, Hyderabad, Navi Mumbai, Noida, and Pune are lesser-known but have most if not all of the qualities of the first-tier cities.[16]

Scenarios for India

As in chapter 3 for our China scenarios, we now apply Gartner's methodologies in scenario planning to identify the most probable paths for India's ICT industry. Again, this framework is provided as a toolkit to track and assess a range of significant milestones and signposts to help sharpen your analysis and decisions.

The three scenario paths identified within the four quadrants in figure 6-2 summarize our view of the realistic range of outcomes for India's ICT industry by 2012. Progress or lack of progress along the two critical uncertainties we've described will determine how the ICT scenarios will evolve. Of the myriad possibilities that theoretically exist for the scenarios, there are only three that are realistic and worthy of consideration. We chart these scenarios as possible paths to the future and assign probability ratings to them, similar to our methodology for the China scenarios in chapter 3.

The three scenarios paths for India are as follows:

1. *Isolated ICT Islands (20 percent probability).* With very limited improvements in workforce capacity and infrastructure, individual companies continue to create isolated centers of IT capabilities. These islands have their own electric power, water supply, and even hotel accommodations. New islands beyond Bangalore, Mumbai, and Chennai are established in cities with more appealing public policies and infrastructure advantages.

2. *ICT Superpower (30 percent probability).* Major investments and policy changes transform educational institutions and urban and rural infrastructure. With heightened potential for

FIGURE 6-2

India's ICT landscape in 2012

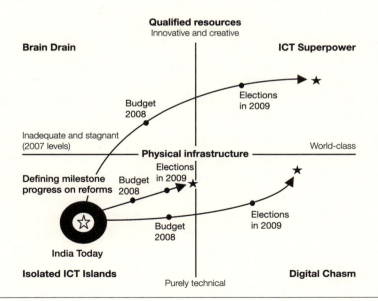

a more highly trained workforce and a modern infrastructure, the ICT industry attracts more foreign capital, generates more innovation, and extends its world-class status far beyond IT services.

3. *Digital Chasm (50 percent probability)*. Significant improvements in roads, airports, power utilities, and other infrastructure brighten physical environments and growth opportunities for the IT industry. Yet, with no parallel improvements in educational institutions, India's ICT "miracle" remains confined to the elite, mainly in urban areas. Fault lines along existing rich-poor and urban-rural policy disputes widen, and economic reforms stall. Today's digital divide becomes a digital chasm.

The second, most favorable, scenario path for the IT industry traces an arc beginning at the "India Today" star in the lower-left quadrant, "Isolated ICT Islands," and moves through the upper-left quadrant, "Brain Drain," before landing in the upper-right quadrant, "ICT Super-power." We believe the Brain Drain scenario path is not very likely, although elements that could create such a future for the IT industry do exist.

We do not directly address the Brain Drain scenario elsewhere in the chapter, given its very low probability. Nevertheless, aspects of this scenario do affect the others; thus a brief definition is in order. In the Brain Drain scenario, India government officials would opt for widespread improvements in the country's educational institutions but continue to neglect the nation's woeful infrastructure in transportation, electric power, water supplies, and other essential services. Thus infrastructure issues would persist as a major constraint in India's economy. Job creation in the IT industry would lag the accelerating pace of world-class talent coming from India's revived academic institutions. Waves of smart, creative, and innovative students leave India after graduation for better opportunities in developed economies.

Despite increasing waves of returning Indians from the United States, the United Kingdom, and other global locations to jobs in India, anecdotal evidence continues to surface that raises the threat of a "back to the future" brain drain. Many of India's most highly qualified graduates continue to be wooed to overseas placements, as occurred in the period between 1980 and 2002. Recruiters from leading global companies continue to recruit quite successfully on India's elite campuses, with offers mostly for positions outside of India in highly developed Western economies, but also in China.

Twenty-one global companies participated in the first round of job interviews for the class of 2006 at the elite Indian Institute of Management in Bangalore. Heavyweight investment banks, all hiring for non-India operations, included Goldman Sachs (hiring for London and New York), BNP Paribas (Hong Kong), Barclays Capital (London, New York, Hong Kong, and Singapore), Merrill Lynch (Hong Kong and Singapore), Lehman Brothers (New York, London, Tokyo, and Hong Kong), Deutsche Bank (London), ABN AMRO (Hong Kong), UBS (Hong Kong and London), and JP Morgan (London). Barclays Capital made the highest accepted offer—$195,000 for a London posting. It was exceeded a few weeks later when an unnamed Indian technology firm offered $223,800 to a graduate of the Indian School of Business in Hyderabad, presumably for a position within India.[17] Compensation analysts also report that the salaries paid to Indian MBAs at the first-tier colleges now compare favorably with those being paid for Harvard and Stanford graduates.

Global companies establishing operations in India should gear up for a strong competition for talent, especially for the top talent in the country. Substantial investments will need to build brand awareness in India and on Indian campuses. This effort in India must be focused primarily on prospective employees, not on prospective customers. A good example is the U.K.-based retailer Tesco. Its large billboards across key cities in India promote high-end IT work being done in India for Tesco globally. This has created a strong buzz among IT employees and students about attractive job opportunities available today in India, especially in the retail industry. This is happening at a time of rising interest among IT employees and students in industry-specific, rather than general, IT careers. As a result, global companies recruiting in India have new opportunities to strengthen prospects for future employee stability and loyalty by screening IT job candidates now for particular interest in their industry.

India should not be viewed purely as a provider of low-cost resources, although that is all many global enterprises see. Any company exploring opportunities to base operations in India should have broader criteria in mind regardless of their business plans. This is especially true if an enterprise is creating a subsidiary dedicated to supporting its own internal operations or even outsourcing from India. To be sure, broad-gauged hiring qualifications can be secondary to cost issues when a company is selling products or services in India or hiring staff for local operations. In the latter case, it is imperative, however, to have Indian-staffed and Indian-led local operations as quickly as possible. A judicious mix of local managers familiar with business realities in India and able to integrate the enterprises' global practices in general are essential.

In our view, the central government will not approve fiscal year budgets in coming years committing solidly to educational reforms or to infrastructure improvements. If anything, the government is more likely to muddle along the current path with minor improvement on both fronts. That is the scenario in our "Isolated ICT Islands" quadrant. As noted, we give this scenario the lowest probability ranking (20 percent) among our three probable scenario paths.

Isolated ICT Islands: Back to the Future

The widening gap between living standards in India's cities and rural regions is at the center of this scenario. Clearly, it is the least appealing future for India. In this scenario, India fails to expand the quality of its labor force beyond largely technical capabilities and the country's national infrastructure remains quite poor compared with other developing economies. As Anand Mahindra, vice chairman and managing director of Mahindra & Mahindra, the diversified industrial company, wrote early in 2006, "We stand no chance of becoming a manufacturing power without the bedrock foundation of efficient infrastructure."[18]

India's notoriously poor infrastructure is the reason why Dutch global electronics company Philips is more successful at making light bulbs in China than in India. Light bulbs have to be packaged in corrugated cardboard tubes instead of thin boxes even for local travel. "The light bulbs break when bumping around in the back of a truck along India's rutted roads. Because there are relatively few goods exported from India, sailings from India's ports aren't frequent enough for the global economy," *Forbes* reported.[19]

Bangalore, the shining light of Indian IT, is strangely enough also the city that increasingly represents one of the main problems highlighted in this scenario: poor infrastructure caused by a lack of foresight, planning, and investments. Despite aspirations to become the "new San Francisco," Bangalore is instead a "premature metropolis" that has grown too quickly, according to local academic Ramchandra Guha. "Twenty years ago it was a town of a couple of million people. Now it's eight million (and) public systems simply can't cope."[20] As an IT hub, Bangalore has the buzz of being one massive incubator of innovation. As a major capital, however, it is dysfunctional.

Yet, like Bangalore, this Isolated ICT Islands scenario has its bright spots. There will be localized pockets—or "spikes"—of high-tech innovation. Bangalore itself could be in a good position to benefit from accelerating collaborations between India and China, a potential we explore in the next section of the book. Yet even if this materializes, India's IT industry will remain focused solely on export in the ICT Islands scenario. The domestic market will remain weak, and India will be forced to compete primarily on cost in global markets, as it does today, rather than race-to-the-top capabilities rooted in advanced education and innovation.

ICT Superpower: World Leader in IT Innovation

As is clear from our 30 percent probability rating, we do not expect this scenario to become reality—certainly not within the next five years. In this scenario, India stakes its claim as a global economic superpower and a leader in IT. Its companies are highly competitive in global markets, with rising market shares. Accelerating investments by global companies, primarily in the IT industry, generate world-class innovations and rising exports. Government reforms open capital markets to high levels of foreign direct investment by companies eager to participate in India's growing economy.

Many of India's most talented executives and investors, after several years of success in Western economies, return to their homeland to leadership positions in business, government, and academia. India's trade surplus widens, generating abundant cash reserves. Government-industry alliances collaborate to direct increased spending on priority infrastructure projects and education reforms. Job growth increases. Millions more children gain access to basic education, and adult literacy rates improve. A virtuous circle is underway.

The problems associated with inefficient government and a lack of thoughtful debate about India's future among business, academic, and government leaders also make this scenario unlikely. There is a lack of will among India's leaders to create the necessary conditions for an ICT Superpower outcome. This absence of a collective national will is the biggest missing ingredient. Required elements do exist within India, which is why this scenario is feasible. We have seen the potential for the broader economy in what has occurred in just a few years in mobile telephony. When government takes positive steps to reform industries and open them to eager foreign capital—and foreign competition—good things happen. In the case of mobile telecommunications, the results have been major improvements in service and declines in costs.

Digital Chasm: Stumbling Along with Dwindling Relevance

In this scenario, India remains a reasonable force in global IT markets, but innovation and related economic growth will occur at a faster pace in other developing nations, albeit with important contributions by Indians. India itself will lag. We believe, though not overwhelmingly (50 percent probability), that this is the most likely path for India's ICT industry during the next five years.

The obvious danger to India is that the remarkable gains of the past decade, notably in IT and manufacturing, will have been wasted. Momentum required to elevate more of India's economy into world-class products and services, to be a global leader, will have been lost. Historians will record this period for India as a classic case of one step forward and two steps back, with progress denied simply because reliable infrastructure development and consistent levels of government support for qualified resources did not materialize.

Another potential danger is that global enterprises will grow weary of waiting for India to get its act together and provide a stable and predictable platform for business. They might turn to other countries that are in the race for scarce FDI. In some cases, we could see companies already invested in India pulling out. While this is not a very strong possibility at this point in India's globalization journey, given the long-term potential of India's economy, it cannot entirely be dismissed. We encourage global enterprises to include contingency plans for such an exit, should it become necessary.

Critical Uncertainty One: Infrastructure

Consider the examples of two of India's poorer central states, Bihar and Orissa. Growth in these states has lagged India overall since the 1990s, and poverty is likely increased. Bihar has huge tracts of fertile land and several rivers, yet a viable agriculture industry does not exist because of low investments in facilities and irrigation. Orissa, a popular tourist destination with magnificent ancient temples on India's east coast, has a significant IT offshore services industry, led by operations owned there by TCS and Infosys. Orissa's coastal location on the Bay of Bengal makes it an attractive site for manufacturing, notably in steel, aluminum, and petrochemicals, but these opportunities are lost because basic infrastructure is not in place.

Access to badly needed foreign direct investment is a major impediment to infrastructure development. The obstinacy of rigidly leftist elements in the Congress Party's coalition government strongly limits the far-reaching policy decisions required to further liberalize India's economy. As China has demonstrated, as well as the West Bengali Marxists, Communism per se is not necessarily a barrier to bold steps supporting economic development. But India's brand of Communists in the federal government is a throwback. Since the Congress Party's surprise defeat of the Bharatiya Janata Party in 2004, the Communists have stymied or significantly delayed many reforms advocated by Prime Minister Singh: airport reform, electrical power reform, privatization. Most efforts have been blocked by the Communists.

Even Mumbai, the financial capital of India, has been unable to make much progress toward Dr. Singh's vision to "make Mumbai another Shanghai," a global financial hub with modern highways, high-rise office towers, cultural meccas, and attractive housing districts. The Congress Party–led government approved spending to renovate the Marine Drive along the Indian Ocean, patterning it after Shanghai's famed Bund along the Yang Po River, a focal point of Shanghai's renaissance with landmark towers and a vibrant economic zone. But local opponents in Mumbai immediately swarmed the court system to block redevelopment. A laudable high-profile project that might have made an important statement to the global business community now seems certain to languish for a few years. At best, a compromise will be reached and some aspects of the project will move forward. In India, compromise agreements achieved in the courts may appease various stakeholders, but typically they yield watered-down programs that bear few elements of original plans.

The level of infrastructure needed to sustain a Digital Chasm path can be achieved by the private sector without much initiative from government. When the private sector cannot do the job on its own, focused pressure by industry associations or company management on *local* politicians often delivers some relief. But in the main, India's business leaders can only fantasize about what it would be like to have an infra-structure campaign of epic proportions, coordinated and driven centrally by government-industry partnerships to prevent India from falling further behind China.

Critical Uncertainty Two: Qualified Resources

India's elite academic institutions, the Indian Institutes of Technology (IIT) and the Indian Institutes of Management (IIM), provide, among other valued services, a recruiting system that many of the world's leading corporations, think tanks, and academic institutions find irresistible. Graduates of the schools typically scored in the ninety-eighth percentile or higher on admission tests, overcame odds that reject more than nine hundred ninety of every one thousand applicants, and completed rigorous course work reputed to combine process discipline, cutting-edge knowledge, and creative analysis.

The seven IIT campuses and six IIM campuses together mint fewer than five thousand graduates a year. Few would dispute the commercial value of these diplomas. Top salary offers frequently exceed $160,000, roughly equal to those offered to the Harvard, Wharton, Stanford, and other top graduate U.S. business school graduates.

For CIOs, business strategists, or decision makers that have India in their sights, understanding the stature and influence of these publicly funded institutions in Indian industry and society is very important.[21] Most Indian politicians consider these institutes a wellspring of great national pride and of optimism for the future. China eyes them with unabashed envy. The institutes are one world-class achievement of Indian society that Chinese leaders are determined to replicate in their country. Expanded slowly by the government after the first IIT opened in 1951 and more actively in the past decade, these Indian academies have stood as something of a national wonder—beacons of intellectual excellence and integrity in an ocean of poverty and illiteracy. Praised by India's first prime minister, Jawaharlal Nehru, as "India's future in the making," the IITs have maintained unwavering support of politicians who otherwise devoted few resources to educating India's masses for the past half century.

One might think that Indian politicians would want to keep the proven success formulas of IIT and IIM intact. Yet, the most bracing parliament debate in India in the summer of 2006 (March and April) was not about how best to expand the influence of these institutions more broadly across India's system of higher education, as many IT leaders had advocated and anticipated. Surprisingly, the debate was about restructuring the system in a way that India's IT leaders cannot approve. Essentially, the government asked the question, If *fewer* of India's best-educated, brightest students have access to India's superior technology and business academies and *more* of India's students from the underprivileged castes take their places, but without regard to merit, will India's economy and society benefit or lose? Their answer was that such a change would benefit society.

In May 2006 the central government approved a law stating that *half* of all students admitted to IIT and IIM henceforth would be members of specific castes and disadvantaged tribes. The previous quota had been 22.5 percent, although experience over several years showed that fewer than 10 percent of these "reservation" seats often were filled. (Note to U.S. readers: "reservation" in India has a connotation and political correctness similar to "affirmative action" in the United States.) Dropout rates, predictably, were far higher among quota students than nonquota students. On average, these "reservation" students tested 10 to 40 percentile points lower than nonquota applicants, who scored at the ninety-eighth percentile or higher.

The caste system has long been seen from the West as almost synonymous with India and Indian culture, but there are a lot of myths about what it is and what it is not. In ancient times, castes were designated for roles or "careers." The system degenerated over the centuries into sorting people from high and low social status, with resulting discrimination. Today, the caste system is alive and well in rural India but not very prevalent in most urban areas. The only exception to this, unfortunately, occurs when caste-system dynamics are used for political gains, such as in this call for new quotas for lower-caste enrollment at IIT and IIM. Government officials argued that expanded quotas for the disadvantaged and reduced allocations to prospective world-class scholars would open doors for the rural and urban to an elite education as well as to potential future wealth and power. IT industry leaders, aghast, saw a weakening future talent pool—a potential setback to India's global competitiveness, and a half-baked, even cynical attempt to shore up political support in Congress Party rural strongholds. They were quick to oppose the quota expansion. We agree that this policy change has the potential to reduce the quality of graduates critical for the continued, long-term expansion of the ICT industry. We do not anticipate any meaningful near- or medium-term impact.

The dispute highlights the seemingly intractable social conflicts that continue to constrain India's ability to address its shortage of people educated and trained to ignite India's ascent as a global IT powerhouse. We see the dispute as a signpost, confirming for now our view of the digital chasm being the most likely scenario path for India's ICT industry through 2012, that is, a stumbling along with dwindling relevance as socialist doctrine hangs on, while globally competitive capitalist breakthroughs occur occasionally elsewhere.

There are positive milestones and signposts in the Digital Chasm scenario, now evident, that continue to capture the imagination of strategists and executives at leading global companies. Jeffrey Immelt, chairman and chief executive of General Electric (GE), told business and government leaders in Mumbai that he expected GE's revenues in India to double in three years, to $10 billion in 2008 from $5 billion in 2005, and that GE's in-country assets would accelerate even faster, to $8 billion in 2010 from $2 billion in 2005.[22] Power-plant turbines, water-treatment technology, and other infrastructure equipment were at the top of his list of sales prospects in India. The head of the GE Infrastructure Unit, the company's largest division by revenue, said that the Indian government appeared to be more favorably disposed to infrastructure projects following the 2004 elections.[23]

This optimism in part reflects an easing of controls on capital flows in and out of the country. In a related step, the government also appeared to advocate convertibility of the Indian currency, the rupee, in capital accounts without restriction. Prime Minister Singh advocated the change in spring 2006, and the Reserve Bank of India quickly followed with a roadmap for how the adjustment would be executed. The practical effect would enable foreign investors to inject capital more quickly into India, thereby increasing FDI, with less risk of loss due to currency price fluctuations. The Indian ICT industry, in turn, would be able to grow more quickly through acquisitions beyond India's borders.

The ICT industry is the most aggressive within India in overseas acquisitions. And acquisitions are one route to hiring talent—in effect, buying talent in another company. The IT services firms are the most active, with acquisitions expected to make important contributions to growth rates projected to average 30 percent to 40 percent annually for the next three to five years. In the long term, Indian companies with innovative operations in developed economies will be in a good position to recruit well-qualified nationals.

Another solution to the talent shortage is India's growing popularity as a career-enhancing move for ambitious professionals in global companies. Indian expatriates have long pursued these positions in their homeland. Applications are increasing from non-Indians. Moreover, Indian companies have succeeded in recruiting more graduates directly from the world's leading business schools. These fresh graduates typically are sent to India for a few weeks or months of training then assigned to company operations based in the graduates' country of origin.

The bottom line is that Indian IT firms are becoming willing and effective recruiters far from India. This is important not only for broadening the potential pool of high-quality recruits, but it also begins the process of building a strong bench of non-Indian nationals. If the Indian companies mature into truly global businesses, several of these non-Indians will one day rise through the ranks into senior management. We anticipate that more global companies will encourage rising, upper-management candidates to live and work in India—and China—as part of these executives' grooming process. Global companies in many industries need to understand these growing domestic consumer markets, as well as the markets' impact on global standards, products, and services.

This chapter has argued that India has the potential to be on a path toward global ICT Superpower status by 2012. To improve its prospects, India must make visible commitments and progress in improving its woeful infrastructure, by all accounts the main impediment to its economic and social progress. At the same time, it must broaden its pool of well-educated, well-trained employees and extend the skills of professionals beyond technical expertise to effective managerial behavior and communications.

While ICT Superpower status is a realistic aspiration, government intransigence on the two primary constraints on India's progress—infrastructure and an expanding, well-educated workforce—is expected to continue. For that reason, the most likely scenario path—Digital Chasm—will yield only gradual, spotty progress, with the private sector largely continuing to fend for itself in global markets of widening opportunities.

In many ways, answers to India's problems could lie just across its border. China has the infrastructure and educated labor force that India needs. What if the two countries merged their respective strengths and opportunities into the pan-Asian economic collaboration we call "Chindia"? Cross-border experimentation in the ICT industry is already underway. Longer-term possibilities are realistic, logical, and intriguing. Yet both countries will require political, diplomatic, and business skills that neither has yet displayed. They also require serious, high-level leadership to pursue the obvious benefits.

In part III, we apply the same methodologies used in part I and part II to forecast dual-market scenario paths for the ICT industry in China and India together—"Chindia." Indeed, there are enough early signposts to suggest this unanticipated collaboration across Asia's two largest countries, heirs to the world's largest economies by the second-half of the twenty-first century, might well begin to take shape.

PART THREE

Chindia

CHAPTER seven

The Emerging Economy
of Chindia

W HAT IS THE SIGNIFICANCE of the current level of China-to-India and India-to-China commercial interactions? Where do the two countries stand along a potential path toward a unified Chindia economy? This chapter addresses those questions. Modest steps recently underway provide only a hint of what India and China collectively could bring to the global economy and global balance of power in coming decades.

China and India hardly qualify today as trading partners by conventional standards for industrialized economies. Total bilateral trade amounted to $18.7 billion in 2005—more than twice the 2003 level. This is only a small fraction of each country's foreign trade. China's foreign trade in 2005 was $1.4 trillion, rising 23 percent from 2004. India's foreign trade in the 2005–2006 fiscal year amounted to $241 billion, up 28 percent. Yet the annual growth rate of internal Chindia trade is outpacing those highstepping totals, at an estimated 30 to 40 percent. Patterns of a widening bilateral commercial partnership are visible in increasing high-level official visits and pronouncements, conference participation, cultural exchanges, and, most of all, forecasts of accelerating goods, services, and investment flows across the Himalayas.

China's more prominent companies competing in global markets have made it a priority to overcome their lagging efficiencies. They are turning to India's IT services firms for help. These Indian firms, in turn, are certain to win more and larger contracts in China. They are highly regarded by leading manufacturers and professional services firms in China's rapidly expanding industrial sectors, including hardware, telecommunications, automotive, and pharmaceuticals. Meanwhile, China's manufacturers are increasing shipments of industrial machinery, semiconductors and telecommunications equipment, consumer electronics, and textiles into India as profits and purchasing power in the subcontinent continue to increase.

The numbers are telling. China passed Japan as India's largest trading partner in northeast Asia in 2005 and is expected to displace the United States as India's largest trading partner worldwide by 2007. Business leaders in China and India are mobilizing efforts to increase their bilateral trade beyond $50 billion by 2010.[1] India's IT service and business process outsourcing (BPO) firms will continue to have a major part in this growth. Several leading Indian IT service and BPO firms established partnerships in China with Chinese IT service firms in 2004 and 2005.

From 2006 through 2010, India is expected to add 71 million workers to the global labor pool, with China adding 44 million, according to the investment firm Morgan Stanley. This compares with a projected 10 million additional workers in the United States, no additions in Europe, and a decline in Japan of 3 million.[2] If current trends continue, China's economy will surpass the United States as the world's largest in purchasing power parity by 2015. Within the same time frame, India's purchasing power parity is expected to displace Japan's, in third position behind the United States.[3]

This quickening pace is occurring as both economies improve their rankings in global competitiveness. On the IMD World Competitiveness Scoreboard for 2006, China ranked 19, behind Japan and Taiwan, compared with 31 in 2005. India was ranked 29, behind Germany and Belgium, up from 39 a year earlier. Among their followers were Scotland (30), France (35), Spain (36), South Korea (38), South Africa (44), Turkey (51), Brazil (52), and Russia (54).[4] IT operations leaders, IT business strategists, and decision makers will want to assess potential market effects of these developing collaborations and conflicts: understanding and evaluating what could go right for China and India aligned together in commercial activity, as well what could go wrong, could yield important long-term benefits.

Western enterprises are certainly aware of potential challenges coming from China and India separately, and some are already factoring potential competitive threats into their strategies.[5] "The dominant theme in German boardrooms at the moment is whether a company from one of these countries will one day—say in five or ten years—be able to take over a big company," said the head of an investment bank in Frankfurt. "Nobody feels safe—from Eon and Siemens [the two largest companies by market capitalization] downwards."[6]

India continues to have population growth and is projected to overtake China as the most populous nation by 2010. India's rapid rate of population growth has slowed, but China has reversed its population growth to a large extent with its one-child policy over the last twenty years. The opening of their respective economies—China since reforms initiated in 1978 and India since 1991—to global markets has made hundreds of millions of their workers far more relevant and productive in the global economy. For the first time, what historically has been these countries' single largest burden—massive populations—is rapidly becoming their biggest asset. How China and India combine these assets is bound to be of epic significance to the global economy.

The most globally competitive businesses in India—Tata Consultancy Services (TCS), Infosys Technologies, Wipro Technologies, and Bharat Forge Ltd. among them—are in the Chindia vanguard, initiating serious business partnerships in China. They see immediate cost advantages, massive market opportunities, improving education standards, a more diversified supply chain, advanced infrastructure in place, and the potential to leverage success in China into larger global success. In sum, they see in China a compelling, strategic future for growing their businesses.

On China's side, high-level government officials are the most visible Chinese players in India. They press for more clarity and consistency in Indian trade and foreign investment policies to reduce barriers to greater Chinese participation in India's economy. They see educational and entrepreneurial advantages, hallmarks of established global competitors that have generated a world-class capacity for innovation and efficiency—at least in a few sectors of the global IT industry.

China's government leaders know these are attributes China must replicate to build a more dynamic economy and become more than the world's factory. They see a neighboring nation with a huge and fast-growing population and a middle-class market of 300 million people. India's raw materials—iron ore, steel, and chemicals—also are a strong attraction.[7] For China to achieve equal partnership among the world's economic leaders in the twenty-first century, it must understand how to succeed over time in the new India as well as in the industrialized world created in the twentieth century.

Indian Firms Stepping into China

When future scholars note significant early steps in twenty-first century cooperation between India and China in IT, those taken in 2005 by TCS and other major Indian IT services companies will probably be included. Global clients of the Indian offshore outsourcing firms moving into China will benefit from these and ongoing developments.

TCS teamed with Microsoft and three state-owned Chinese firms to form a joint venture in China, with initial plans to build a large software development center in the southern Chinese city of Hangzhou. Specific numbers for total workforce and yearly budget were in advanced planning stages a year later, but S. Ramadorai, the TCS chief executive, said he expected an enterprise larger than the biggest existing Chinese IT firms, which employed between five thousand and six thousand people. The *Hindu*, India's influential newspaper, termed it "the first really substantial example of cross-Himalayan collaboration in IT" and noted that TCS will be the majority owner.[8]

The new company was created—certainly from the Tata Group's perspective—to closely mirror TCS's established operations in India that provide IT offshore-outsourcing services worldwide. "The key objective of this global initiative is to build the new venture as a role model for the growing Chinese software industry," TCS said when it announced the formal contract signing in July 2006.[9]

In addition to linking TCS potentially to thousands of capable, lower-cost Chinese employees, the joint venture gave TCS a toehold as a well-connected vendor in China's $30 billion domestic IT market. "We can get access to the market here and build our credibility with government backing," Ramadorai told the *Hindu*.[10]

In entering the China IT market with Chinese partners, TCS also created opportunities to expand business in Japan, which it sees as a priority market, as well as Korea and other regional Asian markets where Romance languages are not the norm and in which Chinese companies have strong business ties. An estimated 65 percent of the Chinese software industry's export business is with Japan, although mainly in low-value application development contracts, not design.[11]

"This venture is a significant business opportunity, which is China-centric from a resource perspective, has global appeal in terms of its customer offerings, and is capable of creating a Chinese domestic business of increasing scale," Ramadorai said. He added that the world-class capabilities anticipated "will create new opportunities for IT professionals and the industry in China."[12] In all, TCS planned to hire thirty thousand new engineering graduates in 2006.[13]

TCS was not alone in moving into China. Infosys, India's second-largest software company, also announced in 2005 that it would invest $65 million over five years in building its business in China as well as in new development centers in Hangzhou and Shanghai. The Infosys development centers were expected to employ some six thousand people, up sharply from the four hundred fifty Infosys employees in China in 2006 and more than double the in-country staff of China's outsourcing firms.

Infosys executives see a widening pool of talent in China that is now capable of being tapped for Infosys's global operations. The company planned to hire one thousand Chinese employees in 2006, where wages are far lower, compared with a planned twenty-five thousand new hires within India, where pay scales are rising. Salaries for software engineers rose in 2006 in Bangalore to an average of $2,000 a month, compared with $500 a month in northeast China. "We want to have an alternative location to India for recruitment," cofounder and deputy managing director Kris Gopalakrishnan told India's *Financial Express*. Infosys increased wages in India by as much as 15 percent in 2006, matching a similar increase in the previous year.[14]

Satyam Computer Services, another Indian outsourcing leader, said it planned to hire some three thousand engineers in China by 2007, compared with two hundred fifty a year earlier. A service provider primarily specializing in enterprise resource planning (ERP) solutions, Satyam was smart to partner with Microsoft, one of the most well-established and well-known U.S.-based vendors in China.

Wipro, India's third-largest IT services exporter after TCS and Infosys, moved into China in 2004, setting up a software development center in Shanghai Pudong Software Park, following initial moves into Shanghai Pudong Software Park, Hangzhou Software Park, and elsewhere in the preceding few years by Satyam and TCS (2002) and Infosys (2003). Other Indian IT companies, such as Zensar and NIIT, have also established and increased their China presence.

The first report of a Chinese IT services firm seriously assessing India for expansion surfaced in the summer of 2006. Company sources said Neusoft Group, based in Shenyang in northeast China, was interested in recruiting IT specialists "in large numbers" in India either through establishing a software development center or a joint-venture with an Indian firm.[15] With a staff of eight thousand and 2005 revenues of $63 million, Neusoft is China's largest IT outsourcing firm. Its primary market is Japan.

Leveraging Chinese Resources for Global Customers

IT services companies in India debated and deliberated on their China strategy for years. Their first steps in creating China operations were taken in 1998, well before the Indian firms established their position as reliable back offices and programmers for clients in the industrial West. Subsequent confusion and mixed signals from the Chinese government about foreign-controlled subsidiaries in China were big factors in discouraging further early Indian initiatives and investments.

Yet global clients of the Indian IT services firms—including several of the world's largest corporations—persisted in urging their Indian providers to stay on course with China. In their view, extending development capabilities into China would spread risks in the event of geopolitical crises and, in turn, provide clients options to shift workflow as needed. The Indian services firms today are developing Chinese talent and know-how in the role of trusted agents of their corporate clients. In one case that we know, a large client is requiring its Indian offshore services partner to source a specific percentage of that client's contracted services out of China.

To understand clients' fears of geopolitical disaster scenarios, consider the tense nuclear standoff between India and Pakistan in May 2002. Memories of those days are strong motivators for Indian executives to get development centers, back offices, and even research capabilities up and running in China. Author and journalist Thomas L. Friedman, who was traveling in India at the time of the standoff, portrays the client-provider dilemma vividly in his *The World Is Flat: A Brief History of the Twenty-First Century*.[16] During the nuclear crisis, Wipro's then vice chairman, Vivek Paul, told Friedman, "I had a CIO from one of our big American clients send me an e-mail saying, 'I am now spending a lot of time looking for alternative sources to India. I don't think you want me doing that, and I don't want to be doing it.' I immediately forwarded his message to the Indian ambassador in Washington and told him to get it to the right person." Paul continued, "[I]f Wipro had to shut down we would affect the day-to-day operations of many, many companies."[17] Two years later, Wipro announced plans for its software development center in Shanghai Pudong Software Park. Wipro's focus in Shanghai Pudong is on enterprise resource planning implementation and support, telecommunications, and other projects—all activities once confined to Wipro's headquarters campus in Bangalore.

For Wipro and its Indian competitors, the ability to retain and add profitable, large global client accounts is contingent on their success in diversifying into China and other attractive emerging markets. For now, they can tap into China's potential without relying directly on relatively immature Chinese domestic service providers and resources. This arrangement gives global clients the best of both worlds. Indian service providers' development capabilities, process knowledge, and quality focus, combined with the easy availability of Chinese software resources, will be invaluable to global clients in the medium and long term.

Other Factors Favoring Indian Investments in China

In addition to leveraging resources in China for global clients, we see three other factors pushing executives of Indian external service providers to set up operations in China: (1) expanding services into China's domestic market, (2) establishing a presence through Chinese partnerships in the Japanese and Korean markets, and (3) alleviating cost pressures by accessing China's large labor pool.

Expanding Services

China's domestic market is a potential growth area for Indian companies. Chinese vendors have concentrated on this domestic opportunity to the exclusion of offshore opportunities. Given the relatively unsophisticated processes and delivery models offered by most Chinese IT services companies in an extremely fragmented manner, the world-class Indian companies have opportunities to gain ground quickly in China, either in partnerships or in competition with Chinese companies.

Establishing a Presence in Japan and Korea

Indian companies have long attempted to establish a strong presence in Japan, given the size and potential of the market. Clearly, markets in the

United States and Europe were the priorities and the focus of most of the companies' business development efforts. That is changing, as U.S. and European markets become increasingly competitive and profit margins in those regions come under pressure.

Indian companies have focused on Japan and, to a lesser extent, Korea as key markets in the Asia/Pacific region. The practice of offshore outsourcing is still in early stages there, with the likely prospect of substantial future growth. Yet Indian companies face significant language and cultural challenges that have stymied them in these markets for decades. China, however, has much greater language and cultural affinity with these two economies. By operating first in China, Indian companies should be able to improve their knowledge of the cultural and linguistic nuances required to build effective and enduring business relationships in Japan and South Korea.

Alleviating Cost Pressures

Rising salary and training expenses, talent shortages, and other cost pressures have made even the most efficient Indian IT services companies vulnerable to competitors elsewhere in Asia, as well as eastern and central Europe. It is the price of success, as the Indian companies are well aware. Their strategies are to continually increase the breadth and sophistication of their offerings—to move up the value chain—while looking abroad for lower-cost but talented employees to offload more basic development and back-office work.

China is an obvious choice. As noted in part I, China has one of the world's largest pools of graduating students in the fields of engineering and computer science. It is the *only* country in the world with a scale of qualified young IT professionals to match or even exceed India's. It will take some years for Indian companies to train and develop effective Chinese managers to lead their new operations in China, but there is a strong likelihood that they will succeed. Indian companies have continually advanced state-of-the-art processes for recruiting, training, management, measurement, and resource development for more than fifteen years. These world-class techniques turn fresh recruits at various levels into productive employees very quickly. This is a distinct advantage for the Indians compared with indigenous Chinese companies trying to create a pool of well-qualified IT services employees in China.

Seasoned managers from India have relocated to China to organize and lead these operations and in particular to build training programs. The early movers are starting to show positive signs and results, measured by reduced waste and higher quality. Indian companies also are sending recent college graduates to India for immersion in their world-class IT institutes for periods of three to six months. The Indian IT companies realize that many students ultimately may not sign on as permanent employees. Most of those who do not are expected to help build the IT services industry in China. Many will be direct future competitors in the world-class process and quality standards created and practiced by the Indian companies. In the long run, the Indian companies believe, helping future Chinese business leaders build world-class IT skills is a high-return investment.

Critical Mass to Determine Global Technology Standards

As manufacturing volumes and design sophistication improve, India and China together will have the power to create global standards in many industries, and in many consumer products. China has already demonstrated this potential in some consumer products. An increasing number of Chinese companies have stepped into global markets. The best known are Lenovo, since acquiring IBM's personal computer division in 2005; Huawei, in telecommunications; and Haier, in white goods.

In India, innovations and patents emerging from global technology leaders like Intel, IBM, Motorola, and Microsoft are increasingly providing leading-edge contributions to their next-generation products and solutions. These innovations, though currently driven by global and not local companies, also create a strong ecosystem of creativity, innovation, and talent from which future local innovators will undoubtedly emerge.

Early examples of this trend are start-ups like Pune-based Airtight Networks, providing an innovative solution to the problem of wireless wide area network security, and Acceltree Software, another Pune-based start-up, providing an innovative platform to deploy corporate IT applications to the mobile platform. These companies, as well as long-established ones, have opportunities to exploit unprecedented scale and buying power in China and India to create Chindia-centered technology standards.

Global companies increasingly will adopt these China-India standards or risk falling behind in the world's fastest-growing markets. Within a few decades India and China will be, or will be rapidly approaching the status of, the largest markets of global demand in many sectors of consumer electronics. Many economists project that China will become the world's largest economy in absolute GDP terms (not just purchasing power parity) by 2050 and that India, with its higher birth rate, will ultimately pass China in GDP before the end of the century.

IBM and General Electric, two of the world's largest corporations, continue to accelerate investments and operations in the region. IBM, India's largest multinational employer with 43,000 employees (out of 329,000 worldwide), said in June 2006 that it would invest an additional $6 billion by 2009.[18] A week earlier, GE raised its sales forecast for India to $8 billion a year by 2010, up from $1 billion in 2005, and indicated that sales in China should approach $10 billion "in the next four or five years"—twice the $5 billion it recorded in 2005.[19] Chief executive Jeffrey Immelt expects that 60 percent of GE's new revenues will come from developing markets by 2015, mainly India and China. Both markets, he asserts, "are growing rapidly and we see both as having great potential."[20]

Like IBM, Microsoft is one of many global IT leaders broadening offerings in India. Aware that India has more than thirty-six major languages, Microsoft understands that it must translate its products into more and more of these languages to further accelerate its growth in India. Major investments are already in place to create these local language products in some key markets. Of course, this is not a new strategy. Investment in localized products has long been the case for major global IT companies operating in China, including Microsoft. English is not widely spoken in China. Global companies seriously interested in building businesses there have had no choice but to customize products.

Consider what is happening in mobile phones. Within a span of six weeks in 2006, the important roles India and China play in the global mobile phone industry were evident in different announcements by four key market participants—Mitsubishi, Samsung, Nokia, and Motorola.

Mitsubishi became the third Japanese company, after Toshiba and Panasonic, to signal withdrawal of its products from the fast-moving, fast-growing Chinese market. Mitsubishi executives said privately they also would close a manufacturing plant in Hangzhou. In addition to fierce competition, the Japanese companies lagged rivals in entering China and did not pursue local product adaptations for the China market to match European and U.S. rivals.

On the same day, Korea's Samsung Group—one of five leading global manufacturers that collectively hold 80 percent of worldwide sales—said it would build its largest mobile handset manufacturing plant outside of Korea in Tianjin, in northern China. The investment would be through a well-established joint venture in China, expanding its annual investment more than six times to $197 million. Production in China would expand to 42 million global system for mobile communications (GSM) sets per year, from 24 million, with annual sales for the joint venture projected to reach $4.6 billion.

The next month Jorma Ollila, chief executive of the world's leading mobile phone manufacturer, Nokia, said that his company was within reach of achieving a commanding 40 percent share of the global mobile market after building its share by three full points to 35 percent in the first three months of 2006. This was a head-turning statement for an executive whose company had been in danger of having its global market share dip below 30 percent two years earlier.

Why the optimism? Soaring demand in India and China was a big factor. Gartner's Mumbai-based mobile analyst Kobita Desai has forecast that mobile phone penetration in India likely will reach 32 percent of India's total population by 2009, surging from 6.9 percent in December 2005. This will require distribution and sales of at least 250 million wireless handsets in India alone during these five years. In 2006 mobile phone demand in India was generating 4 million new subscribers each month. New distribution and production technologies are making this possible. As a result, network coverage will expand across more territory in India, and prices will fall as service delivery and mobile phone production becomes more efficient.

Global giants like Nokia have major advantages over smaller manufacturers in the vast emerging markets of India and China because they are better able to establish and maintain costly distribution networks. In 2005 Nokia sold nearly triple the number of wireless handsets of any competitor in India, dominating rivals with more than 60 percent of that market. In 2006 it broke ground on a $150 million handset manufacturing plant near Chennai. Motorola, a distant second in sales to Nokia in India, followed with plans to invest $100 million in a handset plant nearby.[21]

"Nokia continues to excel in the Indian market," says Gartner's Desai. "It has a robust and wide distribution channel network, and continues to invest in building and sustaining a strong brand image. This is a good strategy because new subscribers increasingly are people with lower disposable income who live in smaller towns and cities. Even so, competition is accelerating."[22] Taking account of these market dynamics, it is easy to understand why Nokia's Ollila was so optimistic in 2006. "It is still possible to increase market share," he said, referring broadly to the global market. "The share of the five biggest (manufacturers) has increased all the time. This is a very significant trend. Volumes have grown and the products have become increasingly complex, which strengths the position of the market leader."[23]

Bilateral Trade Networks: The Sino-Indian Cooperative Office

In our experience, Indian and Chinese executives and government officials need to spend a lot of time together before they become comfortable with one another, listen attentively, and stop talking past one another. Bilateral trade networks offer conditions that break down cultural barriers and foster the personal relationships and, eventually, trust required to step together into the unknown.

The Sino-Indian Cooperative Office (SICO), for example, convened in Beijing for its first meeting in 2005. It is a rare business-to-business council specifically for Indians and Chinese. One of the authors, Jamie, attended the conference, helped frame the agenda, and counseled the participants. During that meeting, one of China's influential Communist Party officials, Liu Qi, hosted several keynote speakers at a party-owned lakeside resort outside Beijing, Kuan Gou. It was a good illustration of one group of Asians hosting another in grand style, with prominent officials presiding, putting relationships before business. The resort setting sent a strong signal to participants of how highly Chinese government leaders regard their opportunities with India.

Liu Qi, onetime mayor of Beijing and now its Communist Party leader, gained wide praise for leading China's response to the SARS epidemic in 2004. He subsequently was named leader of the Beijing 2008 Summer Olympics Committee. Liu is one of the main Chinese leaders accountable for creating state-of-the art infrastructure and IT capabilities that will help define how the world views China as a modern, developed country. When U.N. Secretary General Kofi Annan toured Beijing's Olympic venues one afternoon in the spring of 2006, Liu Qi served as China's official host.

Many participants in this and other China-India business conferences sponsored by SICO and NASSCOM said that the most valuable sessions were private meetings to explore potential collaborations between individual Indian and Chinese companies. We remain encouraged. But these relationships are still quite new. Public disputes are inevitable.

In March 2006 China voiced its displeasure with what it considered India's bureaucratic obstruction of Chinese business ventures in India. The Beijing government counted more than 90 antidumping charges Indian businesses had filed against Chinese goods and noted that India still had not conferred "market economy" status on China. A Chinese Ministry of Commerce spokesman cited "India's frequent investigations on our products exported to India, such as antidumping investigations, investigations on safeguard measures," and other procedures.[24]

The complaint in Beijing seemed timed for negotiating impact in India. The Chinese commerce minister, Bo Xilai, was visiting New Delhi then on his first official foreign visit of the year. "Choosing India as the destination country indicates that China attaches great importance to the Sino-India bilateral economic and trade cooperation," the ministry spokesman said.[25] It was the first face-to-face meeting of Chinese and Indian commerce ministers in six years. Minister Bo and his counterpart, India's union minister for commerce and industry, Kamal Nath, agreed, among other things, to pursue a regional trading pact and to establish, before year's end, a CEO forum for Indian and Chinese business leaders.

China Needs a "Chasscom"

China's business leaders have a lot to learn, and gain, from India's commercial networking groups. India's IT services and software industry has benefited greatly from the sophisticated research and lobbying efforts of NASSCOM, which has been particularly effective over the years in blunting potentially damaging new laws and other political maneuvers by left-leaning voices in India's parliament.

China, however, has had a quite different problem. Chinese IT enterprises historically have been local, not regional or national, which typically encouraged stable, reliable support from local government and state-owned banks. Nationwide industry trade associations, professional societies, and other networks have been slow to emerge. The recent creation of SICO was an important first step to encourage leading IT companies, researchers, and government officials to focus on export markets.

We see no evidence yet of SICO and NASSCOM working together on a focused mission to create a Chindia economy. In part this is because SICO's Chinese membership is primarily centered in Beijing: it is not a national delegation. The Indians in SICO are a national delegation, and

NASSCOM is a national organization. Chinese participants in SICO carry the priorities of leading IT companies and government officials in Beijing but rarely those of other Chinese cities. When SICO events are planned, the scope of the business agenda is limited to issues and opportunities of interest to the Beijing members. India's SICO participants, on the other hand, reflect a broad sampling of India's IT software and services companies. They often have a global marketing perspective.

To more effectively benefit from the considerable talent and resources in India's NASSCOM, China needs a "Chinese Association of Software and Service Companies," or a "Chasscom." (As noted in chapter 3, our references to a Chasscom in this book are meant to be symbolic and semantic only. We do not necessarily suggest that China should mimic India and India's NASSCOM in setting up its national body. China's needs may be different than India's, and this should be reflected in any national organization that is set up.) A Chasscom and NASSCOM together could help identify, pursue, and promote economic interests that would help improve global competitiveness and living standards of the two countries.

They also could create forums to build relationships and policy processes among private enterprise, academic and labor institutions, and government agencies. Without these types of focused networks creating links across the Himalayas, progress in India-China technology cooperation likely will be slow paced. It will depend mainly on individual negotiations and partnerships such as those initiated by TCS, Infosys, and Satyam in making direct investments in China.

China, India, the G8, and the United Nations

In addition to their bilateral networks, China and India increasingly will become members with full rights in many organizations that promote global planning, cooperation, and conflict resolution. By 2010, for instance, China and India are expected to be included in the annual proceedings of the industrial economies that make up the current Group of Eight, or G8—France, Germany, Italy, the United Kingdom, the United States, Canada, and Japan, plus Russia. Considering the current scale and growth rates of the two economies, China and India are obvious candidates for inclusion along with Russia in what then likely would be known as the G10.

The G8 summit, since its origins in the 1970s, has focused primarily on macroeconomic management, international trade, and relations with developing countries. Topics in East-West economic relations, energy, and terrorism have been included in recent agendas. Microeconomic issues have also been examined, such as employment, Internet technologies, and commerce.

The United Nations is another forum where India's ascendance, to the equal or near-equal of China's in this case, seems only a matter of time. India has for a number of years staked its claim to one of the permanent seats on the Security Council. Prior to China's qualified endorsement of India, Secretary General Kofi Annan urged the United Nations to add at least six seats to the council to better reflect realities of the modern world. India, Japan, Germany, and Brazil were regarded front-runners for added seats. The United States had not clearly articulated its support by mid-2006. This was interpreted in India as a major remaining obstacle. By mid-2006 the United Nations had not acted on Annan's proposals.

Conclusion

The bilateral economy of China and India is in its infancy. Yet new momentum suggests a powerful relationship is building. China-India—"Chindia"—enterprises will have access to complementary skills and resources and, in turn, will have the potential to lead many global markets.

New joint ventures between Indian IT service firms and their Chinese counterparts are early illustrations of how a formidable Chindia economy could develop. Indian firms bring to the table world-class software expertise and leadership in global markets. Chinese partners have legions of capable, low-cost employees and greater know-how with clients in Japan, Korea, and other Asian countries where English is less prevalent.

World-class technology, global standards, managerial know-how, innovation, expanding populations, low-cost labor pools, fast-growing regional markets—these are the makings of a historic partnership. Yet many challenges stand in the way. The next chapter maps the most likely paths for a China-India alliance.

eight

The Case for Chindia Bloc

T HE IDEA OF CHINDIA—China and India together as a
massive economic and geographic entity with one-third of
the world's population—is acknowledged by many business and government leaders, especially within these two countries. Proponents regard it as powerful and inexorable, a uniquely fated partnership expanding toward global dominance. Skeptics believe that an alliance
will, in the long run, be subordinated by nationalist agendas that can
and will be more often in conflict than in harmony.

Skepticism prevails today in the West, with these reasons often
cited among many noted in this and previous chapters:

- The two countries fought a border war in 1962.

- China dwarfs India with its huge lead in IT manufacturing
  specifically and low-cost, high-volume production generally.

- India's world-class IT services group finds abundant growth
  opportunities in prosperous, cutting-edge clients in the West.

We see Chindia today as an early work in progress, an entity still being formed. Outcomes are far from determined, but early signs indicate

continued movement in a positive direction. Leaders in China and India remember a time, before the 1962 border war, when the two countries traded cries of *Hindi Chini bhai bhai*—"Indians and Chinese as brothers." China's Premier Wen Jiabao repeated it in 2006 while visiting the Indian Institute of Technology in New Delhi. As the economic strength of China and India increases worldwide, business strategists and IT decision makers need a toolkit to monitor their bilateral commercial activities.

These activities are sure to affect end users and sellers of IT products and services worldwide, but how much and how soon has yet to be played out. In figure 8-1, we summarize nine business resources in India that are benefiting early movers from China, and eight business resources in China that early movers from India are pursuing. We also identify five features both economies offer: high growth, inflows of foreign capital (FDI), a global IT presence, global client awareness and interest, and large markets.

FIGURE 8-1

Complementary strengths of India and China

What India can offer China	What China can offer India

What India can offer China
- Services expertise
- Process/quality capability
- Human resources practices
- Help promote the "one China" view
- Global client demand
- Government support "insights" for services
- IT industry bodies (NASSCOM/MAIT) insights
- Financial services and capital markets expertise
- Training infrastructure

(Overlap)
- High growth
- FDI inflows
- Global IT presence
- Global client interest
- Large markets

What China can offer India
- Large(r) market for IT
- Infrastructure for services companies
- Hardware expertise and capability
- Services launch-pad to Japan and Korea
- Global client demand
- Government support "insights" for hardware and semiconductors
- Best practices in leveraging external investment and expertise to improve country's R&D capability
- Best practices in policy implementation

In this chapter, using the same framework analysis applied separately for China (chapter 3) and India (chapter 6), we identify three scenario paths for potential bilateral commercial relations between China and India.

The two key uncertainties in forecasting bilateral commercial activities between China and India are: (1) the progress of cross-border ties among various Chinese and Indian organizations and constituent groups (relationship depth); and (2) the countries' ability to synchronize bilateral, regional, and global policies on major diplomatic and commercial issues (geopolitical alignment).

The vertical axis in figure 8-2 ("relationship depth") depicts the range of possibilities for the China-India relationship. At the low end of the axis, there are almost no interactions between the national governments of the two countries or any of the other constituent groups mentioned above. If anything, the low end implies a hostile state of affairs. At the top end of the scale ("fully engaged"), we have a highly synergistic,

FIGURE 8-2

Chindia scenarios framework (I)

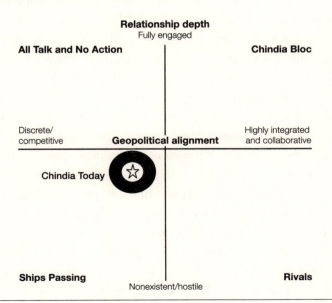

intertwined, and continually strengthening relationship in all facets of mutual cooperation.

These relationships may be tracked at many levels—people to people, industry to industry, company to company, government official to government official, and so on. This is how country-to-country relationships develop in the aggregate. At the national level, interactions may be followed in more detail through separate categories, including government, military and space exploration programs, and R&D activities, to name a few. All these dimensions are essential to defining the ultimate quality of the country-to-country relationship and how that relationship is likely to create opportunities and threats for end-users or vendors in the global ICT arena.

The horizontal axis identifies the range of possibilities in geopolitical alignment between China and India directly and on major diplomatic issues within the Pan-Asian region and globally that affect China and India. The far left suggests a very negative situation—some event or series of events that would equal or exceed the 1962 China-India border war, in which seven thousand troops were either killed or wounded during ten weeks of fighting. The far right indicates a very positive climate, in which China and India are mutually supportive on a wide range of important issues addressed by regional and global councils and governance organizations. This would be similar to the long-standing, mutually supportive U.S.-U.K. relationship. These two countries have disputes but are typically close allies on major issues.

One standard signpost of geopolitical alignment between China and India involves India's long-standing ambition to become a permanent member of the United Nations' most powerful body, the Security Council. China, one of five permanent members, opposed India's bid for decades after the 1962 war. In 2005 China announced qualified support—membership for India without veto power. If China were to support India's full membership, including veto power, that would demonstrate high geopolitical alignment.

The "Chindia Today" star at the center of the circular band, is positioned near the midpoint of the figure, in the upper right corner of the "Ships Passing" quadrant. This reflects how far Sino-Indian ties have improved since India initiated liberalization reforms in 1991. At that time, the star would have been placed near the far left-lower corner of the same quadrant, signifying lower relationship depth and lower geopolitical alignment.

The circular band represents the first major milestone—the Beijing 2008 Summer Olympic Games—along three probable scenario paths the two countries together as Chindia are likely to follow by 2012. Chapter 3 described many reasons why this milestone is paramount for charting China's probable post-Olympics path. It follows then that the Beijing Summer Olympics will be the first milestone as well for charting the path of China and India together.

To summarize, the width of the band represents an extended period underway after Beijing's being awarded the Olympics in 2001 and lasting for several months after the games' scheduled closing ceremonies in August 2008. A successful Olympics in the eyes of Chinese Communist Party leaders would open the door to more gradual political and economic reforms in China and set the stage for more collaboration between China and India. A failure, with high-profile confrontations involving police, military, or policy crackdowns that embarrass the Chinese government in the eyes of the world, would cause major setbacks in China's engagement with the world, including India.

As with China and India separately in chapters 3 and 6, respectively, three scenario paths summarize our view of the realistic range of outcomes for potential China-India collaboration:

1. *All Talk and No Action (10 percent probability)*. In this scenario, leaders in both countries make some significant pronouncements, but there is limited follow-through on issues such as on long-standing border disputes. Modest flows of capital, goods, and services continue, but the rapid rate of growth in bilateral trade decelerates. Advocates for freer trade and economic liberalization founder amid persistent internal opposition.

2. *Rivals (30 percent probability)*. China tightens access to its markets and controls over large pools of capital and physical resources, while India maintains protectionist tariffs and related

bureaucratic roadblocks to Chinese investment. Joint research and academic programs are limited. Intellectual property is closely guarded, not shared.

3. *Chindia Bloc (60 percent probability).* The Chindia advantage builds toward unassailable global positions in manufacturing, IT services, textiles, pharmaceuticals, and other industries. India accesses China's strengths in manufacturing, low-cost labor, and capital to improve infrastructure and expand education among rural poor. As economic liberalization continues, China incorporates India's know-how in digitally driven productivity and world-class academies to build innovation ecosystems, create higher per capita wealth, and improve rural living standards.

A fuller discussion of these scenarios is included in this chapter (see figure 8-3), following a further description of the two critical uncertainties for Chindia.

Critical Uncertainty One: Relationship Depth

Figure 8-3 depicts specific examples of how the relationship can develop across many dimensions and at varying levels of intensity and what forms it may take. This framework enables detailed monitoring of the China-India relationship. The vertical arrow, representing degrees of relationship ranging from "nonexistent" to "fully engaged," establishes categories from competitive to increasingly positive and higher levels of relationship—from mere concurrence to cooperative or collaborative. The horizontal arrow establishes categories from minimally structured interactions among people to highly structured, highly strategic interactions involving national security and military issues or policing.

The shaded band that passes from the middle left to lower right highlights the approximate current state of affairs between China and India across these many dimensions. In the "people" category, for example, India's Prime Minister Singh and China's President Hu exchanged respectful New Year's letters declaring 2006 as "India-China Friendship Year." In "politics" the two leaders scheduled visits to each other's country. Cultural exchanges and negotiations on specific trade policies were explicit or implicit elements of the friendship year agenda.

The shaded triangle identifies a period of limited or negative encounters between the countries, characterized by distant, wary diplomacy between China and India during much of Mao Zedung's leadership of the People's Republic of China (1949–1976), Jawaharlal Nehru's leadership of India (1947–1964), and subsequent governments through the mid-1980s.

The unshaded area at the top half of the figure (and extending below the midline toward the right) represents increasing levels of collaboration and alignment. Activities evident in 2006—portents perhaps of

FIGURE 8-3

Chindia relationship depth

Relationship	People	Politics	Policy	Patterns (of trade)	Patents (science)	Policing (military)
Fully engaged	Free flow of people		Aligned foreign policies	Free-trade agreement	Joint nuclear research	Joint exercises
	Preferential visas	Central bank coordination	Aligned economic policies	In top 3 trading partners	Joint space program	Shared intelligence
	New transit routes	Common positions on international bodies (e.g., UN)	Language education	Shared ownership of resources	Scientist and student exchanges	Military coordination and personnel exchanges
	Growth in direct flights			Large investments	Joint R&D in ICT	
	Tourism grows					Shared security
	"Friendship" year	Mutual trust	Stated policies relating to each other	Important trading partners	Agreement on standards	Military delegations visit
		Leaders visit		Specific trade policies with each other	Aligned R&D initiatives	
	Cultural exchanges					Reduction of forces
		Delegations visit	No stated policy about each other	Basic products		Build-up on borders
Nonexistent/hostile	Few direct links	Fear and suspicion		Low volumes	Each pursues own agenda	

Levels of relationship

expanding collaboration—included rising tourism, discussions of joint military exercises and space exploration, language education, and business partnerships that feature shared resource ownership.

Bilateral Activities Increase in Politics, Economics, and Culture

Several specific events in 2005 and 2006 fit the Chindia framework. They support our view that interactions between the two countries, including many cross-border conferences and research forays, are accelerating, with an overall positive effect on the Chindia dynamics. Major commercial events are reviewed extensively in the next chapter. A partial list of some high-profile events and activities follows, each classified according to a specific category occurring in the figure:

- Indian Prime Minister Manmohan Singh and China's President Hu Jintao issued proclamations designating 2006 as "India-China Friendship Year." In his 2006 New Year message to the people of India, Prime Minister Singh said, "We are confident that in the New Year, we will be able to continue, with greater determination, to impart further depth and substance to our rapidly growing ties, and add an important new chapter to India-China friendship."[1] President Hu said that India-China friendship was important for promoting "peace, stability and development in Asia and the entire world."[2] (*People: "Friendship Year"*)

- Chinese President Hu and Indian Prime Minister Singh scheduled visits to each other's country. (*Politics: Leaders visit*)

- The Indian defense minister visited China; both countries agreed to continue cooperative exchanges at various levels, including transborder visits and sporting activities between the two armies. (*Policing: Military delegations visit*)

- Joint military exercises among India, China, and Russia were conducted. (*Policing/Joint exercises/Shared intelligence*)

- The second volume of *Across the Himalayan Gap: An Indian Quest for Understanding China* will be published jointly by the India International Centre, the Indira Gandhi Centre for National Art, and Beijing University in China. (*People: Cultural exchanges*)

- Film festivals are hosted in each other's country and joint production of films is encouraged. (*People: Cultural exchanges*)

- Literary classics will be translated. Workshops on education cooperation among major universities will be organized in both countries. (*People: Cultural exchanges*)

- An Indian tourism seminar, an Indian fashion show, a food festival, and a photography exhibition will be held in China. India's Ministry of Tourism will launch a Chinese language Web site. (*People: Cultural exchanges*)

Since 2004, the pace of activity has accelerated markedly across many dimensions, including high-level visits by trade delegations, military exchanges and joint exercises, and progress on long-standing border disputes.

There also have been serious first steps between Indian ICT and Chinese ICT industry leaders. Several Indian companies have initiated and completed joint ventures, known as wholly foreign-owned enterprises (WFOE, pronounced "woof-ee") in China. For its part, the Chinese ICT industry has become more aware of market opportunities in India. They are also more focused on obtaining productivity-enhancing capabilities of India's software services and BPO firms. The Chinese are learning the way from Beijing to Bangalore, and from Shanghai to Chennai.

For example, a large contingent of executives from Chinese IT services providers and Chinese government officials participated in the 2006 global conference in Mumbai organized by India's IT industry trade association, NASSCOM. This was a first for the Chinese. We were not surprised when they told us at the conference's conclusion that they were eager to pursue contracts with Indian firms.

In other ways, we have personally observed many vignettes that speak of growing interest in Indian commerce and culture among many

Chinese, even outside technology circles. When Partha walked into a four-story clothing store during a 2006 trip to Chongquing's popular Chaotianmen shopping district, he was greeted enthusiastically by shopkeepers. *"Indu! Indu!"* (Chinese word for India) they exclaimed when Partha confirmed their hunch that he was an Indian national. "Yes, software, software," they added in English, smiling. "Very good!" When Partha stood at the Great Wall outside Beijing a few days later, he encountered many Chinese eager to have their photographs taken with him. India's new reputation for world-class IT services has conferred a kind of exotic star quality on Indian IT professionals in the eyes of some Chinese. This certainly was not the case a few years ago.

In India, you can find a similar affinity for China and the China story. There is a mainstream awareness there of China's remarkable economic progress, particularly its modern cities, highways, and other infrastructure—all of which are sorely lacking in India. It is as if the two peoples are rediscovering each other after a hiatus of almost two thousand years. Historians consider India's major influence on China during that era two millennia ago the spread of Buddhism across the Himalayas. In a similar way, the technology dynamism arising from India will have an important influence in modern China.

A Joint Venture in Chinese Auto Components

A manufacturing pact in 2006 combining specific assets of India's Bharat Forge Ltd. and China FAW Group Corporation is good illustration of a powerful partnership that India and China can create in the twenty-first century. The joint venture is not IT, but its scale, structure, and global strategy provide insight on the current thinking behind these early-stage Chindia alliances.

The joint venture's operations are located in an auto components plant in the northern China city of Changchun. Officially known as FAW Bharat Forge (Changchun) Ltd., the venture employed seventeen hundred workers when it opened in March 2006. Bharat Forge's *control-*

ling stake represented 52 percent ownership of the joint venture. The size was not disclosed, but Bharat Forge described the joint venture as creating the largest forgings company in China.

Bharat Forge certainly is very familiar with market leadership and large scale in India. It is India's largest forgings company, supplying more than 80 percent of demand within India for axle components and engine components. It is the world's second largest forging company, after Germany's ThyssenKrupp AG, headquartered in Düsseldorf. Its agreement with China's FAW was another step in Bharat Forge's strategy to become a components supplier to the world's leading auto companies in markets around the world. From its headquarters in Pune, fewer than one hundred miles southeast of Mumbai, Bharat Forge had already gained a foothold in the United States and Germany through acquisitions in the prior year.

"The domestic Chinese forgings market is four times bigger than the Indian market, so there is a huge opportunity in China," B. N. Kalyani, chairman of Bharat Forge, said at the Mumbai news conference announcing the agreement. "This joint venture will be the largest forgings company in China" and can "act as a large low cost base for global sourcing."[3]

Bharat Forge is the flagship company of the Kalyani Group, an Indian conglomerate with revenues of $1.5 billion. FAW, with $14 billion in revenues, is the largest automotive group in China, producing more than a million cars and trucks annually. FAW built its business through joint ventures in China in the past two decades with several global auto assemblers, including Toyota, Volkswagen, and Audi.

The ceremony officially opening the manufacturing plant in March 2006 was attended by the mayor and vice mayor of Changchun, the Indian ambassador to the People's Republic of China, and high-ranking FAW executives. In his remarks that day in Changchun, Bharat Forge's Kalyani asserted that this Sino-Indian collaboration will become a major global competitor: "This is a momentous occasion in the history of the two great countries, India and China, as well as the two companies, Bharat Forge and China FAW Group Corporation. We are committed to make this JV a success and I would, together with my counterpart in

China, work closely on transforming the JV into a global player in its field of operations."[4]

The press release issued that day from Bharat Forge detailed the partners' strategy with more specifics. First, build world-class capabilities and market them to world-class customers within China: "The JV will focus on offering its range of products and services to FAW Group Corporation and the other automotive groups operating within China."[5] Second, leverage China's low-cost labor to become the global market leader initially within the auto industry, then expand into related global markets: "The JV will progressively position itself as the competitive cost producer of highly engineered forgings for the international market and also focus on the non-automotive business in the fields such as [sic] railways, mining and construction equipment, steel mills, power plant, marine applications and the oil and gas business."[6] These planned trajectories—short-term success within China and longer-term success worldwide—are quite telling and help to explain why manufacturers with global ambitions conclude that investments in Chinese labor and production must be a core part of their global planning.

Let's look at how the Bharat Forge/China FAW vision fits into our Chindia scenario. In the Chindia framework (figure 8-3), the partnership's aspiration is beyond what we define as within our scope in the shaded band area that represents Chindia today. In fact, it falls better into the box above this band, where "shared ownership of resources" occurs with "large investments."

Critical Uncertainty Two: Geopolitical Alignment

While the pace of interactions between China and India is accelerating on many fronts, it is quite modest by standards of the industrialized world. The steps are barely perceptible when measured against the scale of China's achievements in the global economy during the past twenty-five years, and even for India in the past fifteen years. Moreover, their cross-border contacts, partnerships, and policy agreements are quite tentative when measured against such huge, enduring economic partnerships as the United States and the United Kingdom, United States and Israel, Germany and France, and even China and Japan in recent years.

Significant policy evolution and alignment between the two countries are important to improve and transform the relationship currently developing at various levels into a systemic, planned, and unified Chindia. Streamlined policy actions underway include simplifying and reducing procedures for visa certification procedures, expanding flight schedules, and moving actively toward an open-sky policy that would provide reciprocity for airlines in China and India with minimal restrictions on frequency, seat capacity, and airport destinations in either country.[7]

Chinese officials made several specific overtures to Indian government officials and business leaders during a CEO forum in Beijing in April 2006. It was a platform that particularly merited attention of business leaders across India. Indeed, impetus for the event came not within China but from the Federation of Indian Chambers of Commerce and Industry, India's largest and most influential commercial association, whose members include more than fifteen hundred corporations.

During the sessions, the vice chairman of China's National People's Congress, Shen Huan Ren, invited Indian companies to invest in China's state-owned enterprises (SOEs) by acquiring stakes of companies listed on the Beijing stock market, the Beijing Equity Exchange (BEE). The Chinese government was actively selling stakes in SOEs. Shen also urged Indian companies to list their shares on the BEE.[8] Next, China encouraged parliaments of both countries to focus more closely on economic collaboration. Vice chairman Shen requested that a group of Indian government officials meet soon with counterparts in China.[9] Third, Chinese authorities encouraged India to liberalize restrictions on foreign direct investment. Remarkably, Chinese businesses had invested less than $1 billion in Indian companies between 1991 and 2004. "If the Indian government brings in more clarity to the FDI norms, it will help . . . Chinese companies to do business in India," said Wang Jinzhen, vice-secretary general of the China Council for Promotion of International Trade.[10]

As noted earlier, China's qualified support of India for membership on the U.N. Security Council, announced in 2005, was a dramatic advance in Sino-Indian diplomacy. The decision placed China more solidly behind India on this issue than the United States, which by mid-2006 had not clearly articulated its support for India's membership on the Security Council. In another historic policy change, Indian Defense Minister Pranab Mukherjee signed an agreement—in China—in 2006 to establish and expand military training programs between the two countries. This includes joint military exercises, something we had not anticipated would happen so soon. For two countries that fought a vicious border war with seven thousand casualties a generation ago—with border disputes still simmering—this is a deeply significant policy shift.

Further policy advances that promote cooperation in economic, military, science, and technology require focused, positive efforts in diplomacy. If successful, they would contribute further to conditions that facilitate and accelerate all facets of a deepening relationship we describe in figure 8-3.

Scenarios for Chindia

Against this backdrop of significant developments in relations between the two countries, we now look ahead to 2012. Applying the same scenario-planning process as before, the next step is to review the three most probable paths to a future Chindia introduced above, including key milestones and signposts for each of these paths. (See figure 8-4.)

Progress or lack of progress along the two critical uncertainties already described will determine which path the scenarios take.

All Talk and No Action

In this scenario, a flurry of announcements and some significant pronouncements by leaders of both countries would be accompanied by very little action. Many Chinese and Indians consider border disputes the "last irritant," and indeed these unresolved political issues are of obvious importance to today's military leaders. Should they continue to defend the borders as if attacks were imminent? Political leaders agree that the issues must be resolved soon. Yet in this scenario no progress would occur. Meanwhile, modest flows of capital, goods, and services would continue to move across borders. The rapid rate of growth in Sino-India bilateral trade would slow significantly and perhaps flatten. Advocates for freer trade and economic liberalization would founder against persistent internal opposition.

We give this scenario a very low probability rating (10 percent). However it is included in our analysis because negative outcomes from three milestones could contribute to a halt or a reversal of progress on several fronts. A failed Olympics (see chapter 3 discussion of the Beijing Olympics milestone) would escalate concerns that China's government will turn inward and dust off isolationist-protectionist policies. India likely would fare better than North American or European trading partners in

FIGURE 8-4

Chindia scenarios framework (II)

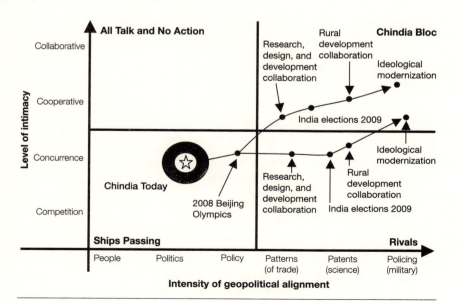

continuing trade and diplomatic relations with China, but even for India further bilateral advances with China would be more difficult to achieve.

In the second milestone, research, design, and development collaboration, interactions between enterprises in China and India would remain sporadic and tactical. No structured industry-to-industry alliances would emerge. China would be unable to establish a national ICT trade organization, a "Chasscom," to mirror India's NASSCOM. Exchanges of government delegations would continue, but not beyond the current existing level of connections in which Chinese city officials independently pursue local commercial projects with national, regional, or local Indian officials.

Momentum for China-India collaboration would continue to encourage the Chinese national government to evolve an agenda for cooperation with India in the ICT industry. Yet progress would be slow, certainly at the national level. Local interests of China's city leaders would be more energized and overshadow priorities of the national government. ICT industry relationships would advance in fragmented ways, but few positive policy initiatives are taken at the national level.

The final milestone in this unwelcome scenario is India's 2009 national elections. It assumes that a splintered coalition government is elected, with Communists and other leftist politicians retaining or increasing power to block liberalization reforms favored by the ruling Congress Party. The Congress Party would continue as the dominant political force, but it would be unable to craft consistent, coherent policy. Officials in India's bureaucracy would continue to send conflicting signals on economic liberalization, with little relief of existing conditions for frustrated investors, businesses, and trading partners. Consensus on economic growth and globalization would recede in the collective political discussion. Fewer opportunities to advance rapprochement with China, such as the India-China Friendship Year theme in 2006, would emerge.

Rivals

To be sure, China and India compete today in many global and regional markets, and in many cases their domestic markets are extremely difficult to penetrate, particularly in manufacturing. Textiles and automotive parts and industrial components are two prominent examples. So this scenario, which we believe has only a 30 percent probability, could become the prevailing direction in their relationship, with a range of trade-offs between negative and positive implications. Isolationist trends after the Beijing Olympics would leave China looking for different allies in a rapidly shifting geopolitical environment. On the other hand, a successful Olympics would produce a more confident, assertive China, and its leading companies would move rapidly to be more visible and competitive in world markets.

For example, Lenovo, currently the third-ranked global brand in personal computers after Dell and HP, could, with at least one other Chinese ICT brand, achieve higher global recognition and revenue impact as a benefit from Olympic sponsorships. China's reputation as an attractive competitor for offshore IT services would rise in tandem with awareness built through Olympic tourism and global media coverage. This could create more competition for India's IT services, but it could also create an alternative, lower-cost source for labor and software development compared with in-country talent in India.

India's ICT industry, led by IT services and BPO firms, would adjust quickly to negative or positive post-Olympics trends, demonstrating goodwill and partnership through both existing and planned investments and related commercial activity. Joint research projects would focus more on short-term geopolitical alignment. At the same time, the kind of new institutions needed to establish trust, intimacy, and commercial breakthroughs with China would remain on the drawing board.

In the second milestone, a forerunner to Chasscom would be organized by private companies in one city, a Beijing or Shanghai, for instance, but bilateral collaboration would be limited to tactical activity among a small number of companies. Little direct government support would be offered or available. Growth rates in ICT activity between China and India would approximate overall economic growth rates in the two countries. ICT patent activity by Chinese and Indian coinventors would be little changed, or it might increase slightly. At least two large Chinese multinational IT services firms would emerge to challenge established Indian companies in China and in international markets.

Next, in India, the election of a protectionist, inward-looking government in 2009 would be a setback for bilateral commerce and diplomacy. China would be perceived more as a competitor than as a commercial opportunity and economic model for India to pursue. Economic growth would be deemphasized, with rural development programs to benefit rural poor becoming ascendant in federal policies.

Milestone four is rural development collaboration in 2010. With rural development a larger priority for both governments in the Rivals scenario, India and China would participate more actively in broad U.N.-sponsored coalitions created for this purpose. They would cooperate on conventional and alternative energy supply projects but remain committed to their own long-term strategic needs. India and China also would benefit from broad U.N.-sponsored rural vaccination and water purification campaigns. They would cooperate to develop innovative and low-cost road construction and housing programs in rural communities.

All these programs would reflect both governments' keen focus on easing social and political pressures rising in the countryside. These pressures brought the Congress Party itself to national power in 2004 and were a main focus of President Hu Jintao's five-year plan, unveiled during the National People's Congress meeting in 2006. Yet pouring federal resources into rural development concerns likely would scale back overall economic growth. For example, in addition to working primarily with targeted U.N., domestic, and regional institutions on rural development, China and India likely would accelerate income redistribution from cities to rural populations and from the wealthy and middle class to the poor.

Ideological modernization 2012 is the final milestone in this scenario. Introduced here for the first time in our analysis, the term implies growing interest among India's Communists and other left-leaning groups in China's Communist-led success with markets and capitalist-style economic growth. This synchronization of twenty-first century Communist ideology with China is already fact in India's West Bengal state, which includes the city of Kolkata (Calcutta) and is attracting significant ICT investment (see chapter 6).

In the Rivals scenario, the two countries would be collaborating in rural development as they attained this milestone. They would probably identify areas where they could work more closely on longer-term development issues. In foreign affairs, China and India would agree on many international policy issues as they focus on more common challenges than on self-interested policy and political maneuvering. Both countries also would participate in selected regional and international university and business programs.

China's twelfth five-year plan (in 2010) and India's 2011–2012 budgets would signal growing interest in bilateral activity, but their funding priorities would remain on tactical economic policy and rural development. The Chinese Communist Party and the Communist Party of India (Marxist) would develop policy platforms independently that support greater Chindia Bloc activity and geopolitical alignment.

Chindia Bloc

This is our most probable (60 percent) scenario for Chindia. Timing trends or events is always difficult in forecasting. Yet if you already travel frequently to China and India, have colleagues on the ground there, or currently live in one of these countries, you can see and hear the case gradually building for Chindia Bloc.

In this scenario, outcomes from the Olympics, whether negative or positive, would essentially be the same as in the Rivals scenario. India's ICT firms continue to expand activities in China, but cross-border commercial activity is more the rule rather than the exception. China would continue to control access to its own vast domestic market, large capital pools, and physical resources. This would force tough decisions on its trading partners and would-be friends, including India. The key post-Olympics questions for Chindia are, To what extent will China need geopolitical support, and how can India monetize its relationship with China in the private sector and at the national government level?

The answers to these questions vis-à-vis the Chindia Bloc scenario will come from new industry, and academic and government partnerships in research, design, and development. The deepening relationship between China and India could become a driving force for the Chinese national government to put aside city-level competition in the ICT industry. Chasscom would be realized in some form, with the Chinese pursuing a stronger domestic ICT industry and technology/knowledge transfer from India.

For India, access to Chinese engineering skills, manufacturing plants, and end-user markets would create a new China focus within NASSCOM that is supported by the Indian national government. Patents would become a stronger measure of innovation driven by bilateral collaboration. With ownership of ICT-related inventions in China and India, patents would be awarded to Chinese and Indian coinventors, and ICT-related inventions made in China and India would increase at least 20 percent. Shared innovation and engagement through the industry trade organizations would set the stage for more coordinated, compatible foreign policies.

In India, the Congress Party would be carried to a resounding victory in 2009. This would end its dependence on leftist factions in forming a required voting bloc to deliver on political objectives of the ruling government. Reform-minded Congress leaders, Prime Minister Singh, and Finance Minister P. Chidambaramas would remain in these positions. They would consolidate political power and gradually enact market-oriented policies. India would move closer to China's approach to globalization. Its domestic agenda would champion economic growth, with continued focus on ICT and other export industries. Partnership with China would expand and become broadly strategic.

In rural development, India and China's progress would advance under auspices of the United Nations and various Asian intergovernmental bodies. Capital resources would increase, partially due to market reforms in both countries that attract higher rates of foreign direct investment. To be sure, social and political pressures would persist, reflecting widening gaps in living standards between urban and rural populations. To address these common problems, India and China would collaborate more urgently on massive rural programs. Priorities would include alternative or sustainable energy technologies, massive rural vaccination and water purification campaigns, and innovative, low-cost road construction and housing for rural communities.

For the final milestone, ideological modernization 2012, success in rural development collaboration would lead to long-term and fundamental recasting of government roles and institutions. Chinese and Indian politicians, particularly in the Communist Party of India (Marxist), would establish new bases of power with their respective electorates. The Chinese Communist Party and Communist Party of India (Marxist) would promote Chindia Bloc activities in domestic and international policy agendas. This would mean little change in China, but it would contribute to a major shift in India toward substantial market reforms.

Conclusion

Chindia is in a formative stage today. Outcomes are far from determined, but early signs indicate continued movement in a positive direction. Bilateral commercial activities deserve to be monitored and taken seriously for potential impact on a wide range of global markets, including, but not restricted to, IT.

The Chindia Bloc scenario, which would favor greater economic clout worldwide for China and India separately as well as together, will be determined by the two countries' desire and ability to create policies to advance their mutual interests. How much they choose to combine resources in research and rural development programs are key issues, as are national trends to be shaped by the Beijing Olympics in 2008 and the Indian national elections in 2009.

The final chapter presents eight priorities that IT leaders and business strategists and decision makers should be addressing now to prepare their enterprises for whatever Chindia profile develops in the next five to ten years. That profile could change the competitive dynamics in many industries and government sectors.

Priorities Today for a Chindia Future

WE ORGANIZED this book into three separate sections—on China, India, and Chindia—to make it simple for corporate decision makers and strategists to assess and address the major implications in the fast-rising economies of China and India for global IT markets. We know that readers of this book engage the global IT markets from many different backgrounds and perspectives—and with countless ambitions. To borrow a phrase from American politics, where you sit is where you stand.

Whether your organization collaborates or competes in delivering IT products and services in global markets, is solely a buyer of IT services, or combines several roles, the national economies of China and India—and of a nascent Chindia—are stirring unprecedented threats and opportunities.

In part I we argued that the biggest uncertainties in China's future are the degree of involvement the Chinese Communist Party–led government continues to have at all levels of the economy and the country's ability to generate world-class innovation. We advised careful monitoring of several milestones, starting with the Beijing Olympics, to see how reality trumps uncertainty between 2007 and 2012. We placed our bet on the China Inc. scenario, concluding that China's economy will continue to make progress, with government remaining paramount but becoming gradually more flexible.

In part II, we argued that the biggest uncertainties for the next five years in India are the government's speed and effectiveness in addressing long-standing infrastructure shortcomings and the nation's speed and skill in improving its educational system for the broad population. We noted significant milestones for gauging movement on these uncertainties, including the Congress Party's interest in continuing market liberalization reforms, spending priorities that emerge in the federal budget of 2008, and the outcome of national elections in 2009. We concluded that the likely path for India through 2012 is halting progress on infrastructure, market reforms, and effective government, with isolated islands of world-class excellence emerging. Yet positive factors exist that could soon transform India into a global ICT superpower.

In part III we turned to Chindia, a story that is more conceptual than real and more speculative than practical in 2007. Many historical and political forces within China and India that could limit its potential may well persist. Yet within the next five years, we believe, economic self-interests within China and India favoring the Chindia Bloc scenario will gather momentum. Some China-India alliances could significantly disrupt competitive dynamics in several global IT markets. This is why we advise IT strategists and decision makers to identify the Chindia possibilities that pose the biggest opportunities and threats and incorporate them into their current forecasting models.

The two key uncertainties to track in forecasting bilateral commercial activities between China and India are the depth of their relationship, that is, how cross-border ties among various Chinese and Indian organizations and constituent groups will move forward, and geopolitical alignment, that is, how well the two countries synchronize bilateral, regional, and global policies on major diplomatic and commercial issues.

The 2008 Olympics, federal budget priorities set in Beijing and New Delhi, and outcomes of the Indian national elections in 2009 are major milestones that lie just ahead. They will affect the shape and timing of the Chindia story. Our view is that the Chindia Bloc scenario will continue to advance. In ten years, a strategic cross-transfer of complementary skills and resources could produce unassailable positions for China-India alliances in many global markets in manufacturing, IT services, textiles, pharmaceuticals, and other industries.

This scenario, however, requires that economic liberalization continues in both countries. If it does, then China and India will acquire higher per capita wealth and improved rural living standards faster than many believe possible. Indeed, the Chindia scenario's evolution is certain to influence progress separately in China and India. A steady realization of a Chindia Bloc would accelerate China's evolution into China Inc. and perhaps even lift India out of its Digital Chasm and into a state of ICT Superpower. Setbacks in the Chindia Bloc could turn China toward Isolation/Protectionism—and India deeper into the Digital Chasm.

Eight Priorities to Focus On Now

Given these three most probable scenarios, and keeping in mind the key uncertainties, we conclude with eight priorities for planning and operations—with corollary action steps and competencies to help strategists and decision makers prepare for whatever realities in China and India develop between 2007 and 2012.

1. Government Policy Formulation by Industry

Action: Engage appropriate government agencies and trade organizations to enter communities and build relationships.

Competencies:

- Local relationship management

- Long-term investment perspective and employment policies and hiring models that ensure industry specific presence

As India and China move independently and together, as we anticipate, toward favoring market economies, opportunities and potential benefits in political lobbying cannot be underestimated. The best lobbying strategy is to support what most officials and citizens will see as good public policy, not to be perceived as pursuing policy changes, or worse, public funds out of transparent self-interest.

In India, for example, Wal-Mart's mantra to encourage political reform to open the retail sector to more foreign investment and competitors was that reform would create many thousands more direct jobs in new stores and significantly more indirect jobs through their network of suppliers than would be lost from some consolidation of small mom-and-pop stores that currently dominate the industry. The ruling Congress Party supports the reform, which bodes well for Wal-Mart. Leftist politicians in the coalition held Wal-Mart and the Congress Party at bay, though, through mid-2006, supposedly defending the status quo for small shopkeepers with procedural stonewalling. The ongoing battle is seen as a litmus test for further liberalization reforms across many industries.

In China, Microsoft was influential in helping the Beijing government establish the Sino-Indian Cooperative Office (SICO) in 2005. SICO (described in chapter 7) is a first attempt to bring Indian and Chinese business leaders together, as well as Chinese government officials, in a cross-border trade association to advance ICT industry issues in both countries. Present at the creation, Microsoft enhanced its political capital in Beijing and its relationships with key businesses involved in SICO.

Partnering with indigenous Chinese or Indian companies is a strategy some smaller companies without long histories in those countries have used to attract government attention. One model is the partnership that Australia's Mincom, a software company specializing in ERP and enterprise asset management for energy and utility industries, formed with Shenyang Neusoft, a Chinese software provider.[1]

Mincom sees participation in China's energy future as a core part of its strategy. Foreign investment in the utility IT market in China likely will drive adoption of worldwide best practices and leading IT applications. Yet the market has proved difficult for foreign companies to penetrate. Mincom failed in its bid to participate in China's massive construction project, the Three Gorges Dam. Its partnership with Neusoft raised Mincom's profile with Communist Party officials, gave Mincom a local presence in China, and established a distribution channel for the company. Neusoft and Mincom were confident that their pact also improved their ability to attract local and foreign capital.

2. Rural Development Investment Programs

Action: Develop a knowledge base on where government investment is heading by industry sector and create business development plans to participate in these spending programs. Identify and leverage commercial opportunities in rural areas.

Competencies:

- National and local government spending process knowledge

- Government contracting knowledge

- Government relations management

- Creativity in rural channel development

- Pursuing opportunities for microcommerce services

Rural development programs are government priorities now in China and India. We expect governments to invest more heavily in low-cost infrastructure, infrastructure deployment, and education and training on ICT.

In China, occasionally violent and mounting protests in the countryside prompted Communist Party leaders to place rural development at the top of the agenda at the National People's Congress in 2006. Government leaders fear greater social upheaval if more wealth and opportunity in China's growing economy are not generated for the rural poor. In India, a ballot backlash by rural poor who felt isolated from the benefits of India's small but surging technology economy swept far-left politicians into power along with the left-of-center Congress Party in 2004.

Strategists and policy makers should not focus exclusively on Beijing, Shanghai, and Mumbai. Keep an eye on rural markets, which can provide significant opportunity, although they require different product and channel approaches, as discussed by C. K. Prahalad in *The Fortune at the Bottom of the Pyramid*.[2] This is especially important for China. A lot of the action will occur in the rural areas. Unilever and Danfoss are among several pioneers in producing and selling basic consumer and industrial products in poor regions.[3] Unilever India, partnering with Hewlett-Packard, provides basic technology—a single PC, Internet access, and a handheld digital assistant—to villages and encourages questions online to a panel of experts on farming, schools, food pricing, health, computing, and other topics. Answers are delivered verbally, via computer, in local languages. Unilever recruits run the programs—and also sell Unilever soaps, shampoos, and other personal-grooming products. Unilever hopes to recruit 100,000 of these local entrepreneurs and reach 400 million customers in 400,000 villages.[4]

Denmark-based Danfoss, a global marketer of valves, compressors, and motor controls that has operated in China since 1996, found appealing niches at the low end of the market. For example, it had Chinese engineers create a new low-priced motor-speed control for commercial refrigerators that covered the basics of what customers wanted—saving energy and keeping dust out of the machinery. "What stunned us was the size of the low-end market" in China, said Jorgen Clausen, Danfoss's chief executive.[5]

Global ICT companies should evangelize further for the potential benefit of ICT in rural communities. Adapting low-priced commodity technology is becoming a big business. Chinese companies, for instance, buy aging computer chip fabrication plants from Intel and other innovation leaders for very little money. They use output from these plants as processors for inexpensive PCs. As momentum builds to develop and market the $100 laptop, an array of new opportunities for once obsolete technology will emerge.

Nokia dominates much of India's rural market by being close to the customer. Its handset menus in the Hindi language (instead of English), introduced in 2000, were very popular among Hindi-speaking rural residents. (More than 400 million Indians speak Hindi.) Nokia followed with its first Hindi-text input in 2002 and first made-in-India handset in 2003. In 2005 it won a $125 million contract with Bharti Tele-Ventures, India's largest provider of telecommunications services, to manage networks that will expand Bharti's Airtel mobile service into more than five thousand towns across India, essentially doubling Airtel's coverage.[6]

"To sustain India's economic, growth, it is imperative to take the benefits of mobile communications to the rural customers," said Bharti Tele-Ventures executive Manoj Kohli. Nokia's country director in India, Ashish Chowdhary, added, "This expansion reiterates Nokia's commitment to India, fulfilling our promise to bring high-quality equipment and services to provide world-class mobile services to the Indian customers."[7] Motorola, a distant second to Nokia in India in handset market share, is trying to play catch-up in the countryside (as noted in chapter 7). In 2006 Motorola announced a new $100 million manufacturing plant outside Chennai, not far from a $150 million Nokia plant already operating.

3. Research, Design, and Development

Action: Build local research, design, and development capabilities through local hiring and investment. Develop strategic technology- or service-based partnerships. Prepare proactive approaches to technology transfer requirements imposed by the government.

Competencies:

- A broad set of human resources capabilities, including profiling, hiring, training, and university relations—investor-level knowledge of and insight into local incubator companies and university development programs.

- Development of localized IP protection mechanisms. As historical levels of infrastructure investments continue, major new government spending projects are likely to be evident in China by 2008 (Beijing Olympics milestone) and in India by 2009 (national elections milestone). China alone is expected to invest $300 billion in infrastructure between 2005 and 2015.[8] An array of IT products and services, with telecommunications infrastructure and broadband in the forefront, will be designed into new offerings delivered through the public sector.

Global technology and industrial companies should participate actively in this process. Their patents, proprietary science processes, and country-specific initiatives can contribute in important ways to design standards and program capabilities. Business success will materialize in consulting contracts, equipment sales, and opportunities to commercialize new technologies that advance the governments' design and development programs.

4. Market Development

Action: Recognize that markets in China and India are likely to have very different characteristics, behaviors, and expectations from the traditional developed markets. Plan for significant "bottom of the pyramid" opportunities in these markets.

Competencies:

- Market research

- Local market analysis

- Culturally sensitive product and service development

Foreign enterprises often overestimate or underestimate Chinese spending on technology.[9] In most cases, for example, Chinese enterprises will not pay a premium for foreign software: they cannot see value in the additional premium purely for foreign IP. Companies will benefit from focusing on improving the price-performance ratio. Although China is a fast-growing IT market, enterprises based in China spend less on IT products and services than enterprises in countries with more-developed economies. Annual revenue in China's IT market is less than one-fifth the market in Japan, less than 10 percent of the U.S. market, and approximately the same size as a large U.S. state such as Florida. Automation in China and India has been less a priority because of the wide availability of inexpensive labor.

Foreign enterprises often underestimate the consumer technology market in China. China is the world's leading market for mobile handsets, the world's second largest market for PCs, and by 2007 it is expected to become the world's largest market for Internet subscribers. Yet e-commerce growth will be slow because few Chinese online users have credit cards, and disposable income is low. Moreover, many companies are required to agree to various government demands for approved access to consumers. These can include investments, technology transfer obligations, and commitments to include locally generated content.

The immense size and complex cultures of China and India make distribution and marketing extremely challenging. A large and growing middle class does exist in both countries, but, in contrast to developed economies, it is widely dispersed. Many newly arrived marketers are confounded, leaving some to wonder if they are pursuing vast colonies of phantoms—"the mythical middle class." China's modern new infrastructure is limited primarily to its major cities. India's infrastructure is notoriously limited, even in many major cities. In China, the economic rivalry between regions has led some regional governments to impose taxes on products delivered from other provinces.

Whether or not you have made or anticipate making major investments in China and India, your strategy must reflect insight into how future opportunities and threats for your enterprise are being shaped by global companies increasingly active in these countries. For IT vendors, this means putting more emphasis on market conditions in China and India when they design new products and services. General Electric, for example, anticipates that 60 percent of its revenue growth will come from emerging markets, mainly China and India. GE spends between $2 billion and $3 billion a year on technology.[10] Connecting the dots—more GE technology spending will be shaped by market conditions in China and India—makes it clear that GE's technology purchases worldwide will be shaped increasingly by its technology requirements in China and India.

For CIOs of multinational companies operating in China and India, choosing appropriate technology for operations may require unusual trade-offs.[11] If the operations in China and India are autonomous, for example, and not synchronized with global systems, CIOs may want to look beyond global functionality in favor of local solutions favored by in-country IT managers in China and India.

5. Chindia Opportunity

Action: Investigate opportunities for your enterprise to leverage the complementary and combined strengths of China and India for increased synergy and value.

Competencies:

- Knowledge of the similarities and differences between the two countries

- Understanding of the areas of natural competition and cooperation

- Ability to track and leverage the individual government's policies that are driving cooperation rather than competition

India's leading IT services firms—TCS, Infosys, and Wipro, among others—illustrate how aspects of Chindia now offer compelling economic logic to global clients. As described in chapter 7, these Indian firms in large part are acting as agents of clients in developed economies in the West. Clients of these firms are likely already leveraging the complementary strengths of China and India.

Recall that TCS joined with Microsoft in 2005 and three state-owned Chinese firms to build a software development center in Hangzhou, with plans to employ perhaps more than six thousand people. The same year, Infosys committed to $65 million over five years to build its business in China and establish new development centers in Hangzhou and Shanghai. Employment in the development centers was expected to reach six thousand people, up from four hundred fifty Infosys employees in China in 2006 and more than double the 2006 total of in-country staff of China's outsourcing firms.

Wipro opened its first development center in China in Shanghai Pudong Software Park in 2005. Staff size early in 2006 was about one hundred, with plans in place to expand greatly in a few years. "We are approaching it step by step, because we want to be sure we get the right profile of people, we deal with the right customers, and we get a reasonable amount of stability in our work force," said Azim Premji, Wipro's chairman and chief executive.[12]

Some Chinese hardware and telecom companies, led by pioneering Huawei, have many Indian developers in their software R&D centers. This means global clients of Huawei often could be using telecommunications gear supported by hardware engineers in China and software engineers from India.

6. Resource Development

Action: Develop the ability to recruit, train, and integrate Chinese and Indian talent and labor at all appropriate levels of your organization, including especially management talent. Encourage expatriate stints within these countries for senior management candidates.

Competencies:

- Knowledge of the vastly different employment ecosystem, including the employer food chain

- Ability to create customized human resources policies (especially related to compensation) given the vastly different demographics

- Cultural orientation and assimilation

Demographics are destiny. India is expected to contribute 83 million workers to the global workforce; China, 23 million between 2005 and 2010. The figures are about 4 million in the United States and perhaps 100,000 in Europe, according to Morgan Stanley. As India and China further command a growing share of the global workforce, companies that succeed in tapping this resource will have competitive advantages.

To be sure, Western companies in particular need training programs that identify different communication styles in the West and Asia. These programs commonly encourage Chinese and Indian colleagues to be more assertive with superiors in problem-solving situations. (This issue is addressed in chapter 3; related challenges for Western managers in

Chinese factories are described later, in the section, "Cultural Understanding.") For more Chinese and Indians to take their place among the world's great innovators, an instinct to break from the past and act on new insights is essential.

Could this be happening among India's new generation? In an intriguing attitude shift, more top students in India who might have studied and worked in the United States or the United Kingdom just a few years ago no longer believe this is necessary in technology fields. Training programs of IT service firms in India are considered the equal of many graduate management and engineering programs in the United States. With appealing career tracks that often include paid assignment in the United States or other developed economies, more Indian students see no need to leave their homeland and absorb the high costs of a two-year graduate degree program while earning little or no income.

For this reason, we expect that companies will locate more talent development centers in India and China, as the latter carries through on major investments in improving academic standards. Moreover, operations management in India and China increasingly will be designated by major corporations as key assignments for their fast-track executives.

7. Local Expertise

Action: Identify and collaborate with savvy, trusted local advisers—employees or external consultants—who understand how business is conducted at local, regional, and national levels. Establish a clear understanding with them of global practices and laws that the organization needs to conform to.

Competencies:

- Identifying the right resources among the maze of middlemen

- Balancing local cultural practices and nuances with global best practices and legalities

- Understanding the strong regional differences and political influences within the same country

- Developing strong political relationships at local, regional, and national levels

Navigating effectively among political personalities and government procedures in China and India is a dizzying challenge for the uninitiated. Yet it is an enterprise imperative. Proven advisers generally are grouped into four categories. Their ranks are growing and, by choosing wisely, you will come to regard many as valuable contributors to your success. The categories include the following:

- Traditional public relations-communications firms with additional risk management, crisis communication, and lobbying services targeted at government officials and other key policy influencers and opinion makers

- Prominent global professional services firms and academic specialists in management consulting, law, and accounting

- Westerners and other foreigners with strong credentials who understand cultures and business practices in China and India

- Local Chinese and Indians, fluent in English and other widely used languages, who also have trusted reputations among leading businesses and policy makers

China is moving toward a rule-of-law environment, but corruption and political and government interference in the judicial system still occur. This is true as well in India, where the rule of law is a long-standing tradition. Inadequate protections offered by the legal system in China and the unpredictability of the legal process in India often lead foreign companies to settle business disputes through international arbitration. In China, new regulations, agencies, and even entire government ministries are created or reformed as the country undergoes immense changes. Understanding regulatory challenges can be a tortuous process, and protecting IP rights is very difficult. Local officials occasionally have protected successful revenue-producing local companies by ignoring rampant infringements of IP.

For U.S. companies, good legal counsel for sales operations in China is essential. Missteps that cross the line on U.S. bribery laws, if detected, can result in prison terms. The U.S. Foreign Corrupt Practices Act (1977) prohibits bribery against foreign officials, political parties, or candidates for public office "for purposes of obtaining or retaining business."

In business development, monitoring political risks and their potential effects is an important activity. In China, two of several ongoing concerns make the point. First, any rhetoric from Taiwanese government officials hinting at a formal declaration of independence draws swift and sharp warnings of military intervention from Beijing. Second, China has kept its currency, the yuan, closely linked to the dollar. It allowed a minor appreciation in the yuan–dollar exchange rate in 2005 and again in 2006. A rising yuan makes Chinese goods more costly in global markets. This makes investments in China risky, especially for companies that rely on China as a place to manufacture goods inexpensively for export.

If China's trade surplus with the United States continues to increase, U.S. pressure for further appreciation of the yuan will rise. In turn, a depreciating dollar likely would force U.S. interest rates higher. The growing U.S.-China trade imbalance also could spark new import tariffs and reprisals between the two countries. Clothing, furniture, and steel industries all have been affected in recent years.

8. Cultural Understanding

Action: Understand and act on significant cultural differences between the West and Asia.

Competencies:

- Multicultural exposure in the workforce

- Critical mass of "bridge" executives from these countries in key roles

- Management understanding not to impose home-country culture, behavior, and expectations locally

- Ability to take a long term—*very* long term—view

Understanding, respecting, and embracing local culture is a critical success factor for Westerners in China and India. Many Western companies fall short in their plans and aspirations for China and India because their strategists and decision makers, based either in-country or thousands of miles away, fail to understand and adjust to how most people think, behave, and get things done in these two complex cultures.

All the history, analysis, conclusions, and advice we have collected here in *IT and the East* will serve as little more than an academic exercise if you are unable to artfully adjust your cultural dial when applying them. For that reason, our final recommendation is the most extensive. If you fail to understand and adjust to the contrast between analytical, logic-based decision processes in the West and more emotional, relationship-based decision processes in the East, the business consequences can be quite serious.

We start with a cultural assessment framework developed by Nitza Hidalgo, former chair of the *Harvard Education Review* and now professor of education at Westfield State College in Massachusetts. The pyramid illustrated in figure 9-1 identifies three aspects of cultural awareness that can help you recognize and measure your cultural agility in any setting.[13]

The "concrete" level, at the top of the triangle, represents what is easiest to see and the most tangible, such as food, music, clothing, and festivals. "Behavioral" connotes unspoken rules on how social roles are defined and what a person values, such as nonverbal behavior, use of language, political affiliations, role of the family, and gender-specific behavior. Education and coaching on these points can be valuable, but one must live a few years in a different culture to begin to understand it and act appropriately in the eyes of locals.

"Symbolic" is the foundation of cultural understanding. It includes a people's inherent values and beliefs—how they define themselves through customs, spirituality, religion, beliefs, and general worldview. Westerners need to display a focused curiosity, an openness and desire to learn and understand how all these elements vary and blend among the relevant subgroups in their work and social networks. With more than one-third of the world's population living in China and India, thousands of subgroups contribute to these endlessly rich, historic, and diverse cultures.

FIGURE 9-1

Three levels of culture

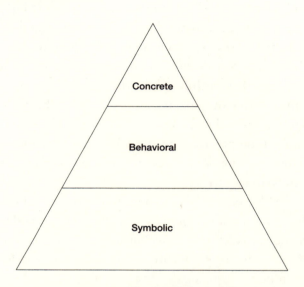

The works of American psychologist Richard E. Nisbett provide valuable analysis of cultural differences between the West and Asia. Nisbett, a psychology professor and codirector of the Culture and Cognition Program at the University of Michigan, notes that Greek intellectual traditions influenced Westerners to emphasize logic to frame and answer questions: "Logic is applied by stripping away the meaning of statements and leaving only their formal structure intact."[14]

India has an ancient tradition in logical reasoning as well, another historical factor that helps place it in a philosophical and cultural middle ground between East Asia and the West—as do the various eras of British influence and control during the past two hundred years. Among other things, the British contributed a national language as well as the institutions of parliamentary democracy and the rule of law in India.

In East Asia, however, a form of cultural reasoning derived from the Taoist yin-yang principle took root. This holds that there "is no necessary incompatibility between the belief that A is the case and the belief that non-A is the case." Put another way, "Events do not occur in isolation from other events, but are always embedded in a meaningful whole in which the elements are constantly changing and rearranging themselves."[15] The Chinese, Nisbett concludes, strive to be reasonable, not rational. His insights on how the two cultures see the modern world differently include the following:

- Easterners are more likely to detect relationships among events than Westerners.

- Westerners believe more that environments can be controlled than Easterners.

- In habits of organizing the world, Westerners prefer categories; Easterners are more likely to emphasize relationships.

- Westerners are more inclined to use logical rules to understand events than Easterners.[16]

The fall-and-rise case of Cummins Engine's joint-venture manufacturing plant in Chongqing illustrates how cultural awareness can be indispensable for Western-bred expatriates leading subsidiaries or joint ventures in China.[17]

Five years into Cummins's equal partnership with the Chongqing Engine Manufacturing Company, formed in the mid 1990s, the plant's performance metrics surprisingly fell further behind what the Chinese had achieved on their own. Cummins was not happy with the joint venture performance and was looking at different options. Cummins brought in a new plant manager, Kirpal Singh, who had had extensive experience in Cummins U.S. manufacturing, building organizations, and improving performance measures.

The new manager kept ROI as a priority, but was more willing to make trade-offs sought by his all-Chinese management team in order to get their buy-in and build trusting relationships. For example, he approved spending programs that exceeded Cummins's conventional standards for payback, explaining to Cummins's Indiana headquarters that longer-term results should justify his roll of the dice.

Kirpal, who was raised in India before migrating to the United States, did not speak Chinese and had never worked in China. One of his first steps was hiring an executive assistant who could be his Mandarin interpreter *and* cultural adviser inside the Chongqing factory. Kirpal held frequent briefings with senior management, which included the local Communist Party leader (appointed the joint venture's chairman by the Chongqing owners), and regular "town hall" sessions before the full workforce.

For many months, the agenda included the basic fundamentals of capitalism. The Chinese managers and workforce often rejected or ignored orders from Cummins's first managing director. They questioned the need for additional profits, so long as the plant generated enough revenue to pay workers' salaries. Kirpal argued that bigger profits would be good for them. Cummins would be more likely to invest in the plant, expand employment, and increase wages. Over time, he won them over. In another two years, Kirpal's Cummins-Chongqing factory routinely was matching or exceeding its financial goals. Kirpal relocated to India for a few years to manage a Cummins plant there, but his former colleagues in Chongqing subsequently recruited him to manage the plant for a second time.

Kirpal told us that the importance he placed on understanding and respecting Chinese culture was a key part of his success. So was his realization that none of his managers or employees had ever worked in a capitalist setting previously. Patience, persistence, and frequent communication marked his approach. He also respected the Chinese preference for long-term factors over short-term results. American businesspeople are known across Asia for their emphasis on short-term operational results and for putting transaction details before business and personal relationships. British expatriates, on the other hand, generally are respected by in-country locals for displaying a broader, more effective repertoire of cultural awareness.

Is the approach Kirpal worked so effectively in China required as well in India? Not necessarily. Making decisions purely in a Western style probably would not be as disastrous in India as it was for Cummins's first managing director in Chongqing. The Internet and other mass media have helped acclimate India's younger generations to Western culture, building on India's British legacies and its own centuries-old traditions in logical analysis. So too have the ever expanding Indian diasporas in the West, especially in the global technology industry. Finally, most Western-based enterprises routinely hire local or expatriate Indians to manage their operations in India.

There are many unanswered questions about the economic futures of China and India, of China and India together, and indeed of China's and India's future impact on the global economy. Can innovation be outsourced? Is it possible to compete in Asian markets without piracy of intellectual property draining away the opportunities? Will China's and India's mounting successes in world markets create a protectionist backlash among developed economies?

We hope this book has given you more tools and confidence to seek answers to these and many other unknowns that matter most to your enterprise as you reassess China's and India's place in the world's twenty-first century economy. The answers you seek may well be among the most important for setting the long-term course and success of your enterprise. The methods by which you pursue them certainly will shape the quality and insight of what you find. As China and India increasingly redefine the future of technology and innovation, knowing how to map a course into that future will be a core competency of the most accomplished travelers.

Scenario Milestones and Signposts for China

OUR SCENARIOS are probable paths to the future. Of course there are an infinite number of possible paths and variations, but we organize the most likely developments into the three possible paths shown on figure 3-1. In this kind of scenario planning exercise, Gartner methodology requires that distinct scenarios should be mutually exclusive and collectively exhaustive. Therefore, when we assign probabilities to each scenario, the probabilities must add up to 100 percent.

The following lists summarize the three scenario paths Gartner has identified for China's information and communications technology (ICT) industries.

Scenario Path One: Isolation/Protectionism (10 percent probability)

Milestone One

Beijing Olympics 2008

Signposts:

- Disruption of Olympics by conflict with Taiwan.

- Trade conflict with the United States.

- Domestic protests triggering highly publicized repression.

Results: Chinese pride is hurt, and its presence and reputation in the global ICT markets are damaged. The country's domestic economy remains healthy, but global competition slows its growth. China outsourcing and IT services progress slows or stops altogether.

Milestone Two

ICT-related patent performance in 2010

Signposts:

- ICT patents as a percentage of total patents slipping to the worldwide average.

- Specialization index for ICT-related patents falling to 80 percent.

- Foreign ownership of domestic ICT-related inventions increasing to at least 55 percent.

- ICT-related patents with foreign coinventors increasing to at least 35 percent.

- Domestic ownership of ICT-related inventions made abroad increasing to at least 25 percent.

Results: Foreign companies continue to create value with their China-based development laboratories but are less likely to manufacture in China due to concerns about political stability. With reduced levels of investment in China, capital becomes scarce and foreign company–driven innovation slows.

Milestone Three

Promotion of China-specific standards

Signposts:

- Declining level of participation in international standards bodies.

- ICT policy focus shifting from export to domestic.

- Increased barriers to entry in selected markets, especially in telecommunications services, handsets, and operating systems.

- Government prohibitions against buying foreign products and services for/by government agencies.

Results: By 2012 China declines as an innovator and global market competitor. ICT remains strategic and becomes a protected domestic industry.

Scenario Path Two: Entrepreneurial (20 percent probability)

Milestone One

Beijing Olympics 2008

Signposts:

- Olympic Games a political, operational, and technological success.

- Lenovo and at least one other Chinese ICT brand leveraging the Olympics for global recognition.

- China's attractiveness as location for offshore IT services highlighted and strengthened.

Results: China's global reputation soars. Chinese ICT companies develop new sophistication in penetrating overseas markets; government policy promotes merger and acquisitions to ensure global scale of operations for ICT companies.

Milestone Two

By 2009 a Chinese ICT national marketing and trade association, modeled after India's respected and effective NASSCOM, is created.

Signposts:

- Precursor to "Chasscom" organized by private companies in one city by 2008.

- Government support for Chasscom grows; more cities included.

- Multiministry announcement of support for Chasscom.

Results: The Chinese ICT industry improves its marketing capabilities through common messaging, trade assistance, information sharing, and overseas market development activities.

Milestone Three

ICT-related patent performance in 2010

Signposts:

- ICT patents as percentage of total patents rising to 50 percent.

- Specialization index for ICT-related patents rising to 1.5 and/or China in the top five worldwide.

- Foreign ownership of domestic ICT-related inventions declining to at least 40 percent.

- ICT-related patents with foreign coinventors decreasing to at least 20 percent.

- Domestic ownership of ICT-related inventions made abroad decreasing to at least the worldwide average.

Results: The pace of Chinese intellectual property creation accelerates as reliance on foreign partners declines. A sophisticated ICT manufacturing base grows, including a semiconductor fabrication industry.

Milestone Four

Reduction in government ownership of private assets by 2010

Signposts:

- Policy shift away from city government ownership of ICT companies.

- At least five major divestitures announced by city governments.

- At least a 25 percent reduction in the number of ICT companies.

- Appearance of at least five $1 billion (revenue) companies.

- International adoption of at least one Chinese-led standard initiative.

Results: ICT markets are made more competitive through merger and acquisition activity. Economies of scale are used to expand both domestic and international operations. Chinese ICT companies establish a global base of operation.

Scenario Path Three: China Inc. (70 percent probability)

Milestone One

Beijing Olympics 2008

Signposts:

- Olympic games a political, operational, and technological success.

- Lenovo and at least one other Chinese ICT brand leverage Olympics for global recognition.

- China's growing attractiveness as an offshore location for IT services highlighted and strengthened.

Results: China's global reputation steadily increases. A small number of Chinese ICT companies develop new sophistication in penetrating overseas markets. Government policy selectively promotes merger and acquisitions to enhance global competitiveness of selected companies.

Milestone Two

ICT-related patent performance in 2010

Signposts:

- ICT patents as a percentage of total patents rises to 50 percent.

- Specialization index for ICT-related patents rising to 1.2 and/or China in the top ten worldwide.

- Foreign ownership of domestic ICT-related inventions declining to at least 45 percent.

- ICT-related patents with foreign coinventors decreasing to at least 25 percent.

- Still above the worldwide average, domestic ownership of ICT-related inventions made abroad decreasing.

Results: The pace of Chinese intellectual property creation accelerates, but an oversupply of vendors still masks market signals. An oversupply of capital continues to be directed into job-preserving, inefficient production capacity. Reliance on foreign partners remains important as a business edge in international markets. New market opportunities are still driven more by government policy than by market dynamics.

Milestone Three

"Chasscom" is created after 2009.

Signposts:

- Precursor to Chasscom organized by private companies in one city by 2008.

- With limited government support, Chasscom membership built company by company.

- Multiministry announcement of support for Chasscom by 2011.

Results: The Chinese ICT industry struggles with international marketing: there is limited Chasscom representation available for overseas market development activities. Lack of common messaging, trade assistance, and information sharing still hinders Chinese expansion into international markets and marginalizes ICT industry influence in government policy development.

Scenario Milestones and Signposts for India

I T LEADERS, business strategists, and decision makers following the rise of India on the global ICT stage should track three potential scenarios in the next five years. Of the following scenario paths, we believe that the Digital Chasm is most likely through 2012 (50 percent probability).

Scenario Path One: Isolated ICT Islands (20 percent probability)

Milestone One

Government reforms progress by 2008

Signposts:

- No major positive policy decisions made or enforced; no progress on ongoing policy priorities: foreign direct investment in retail, airport privatization, and labor reform.

- Enforcement of backward-looking policies such as caste-based reservations imposed on elite institutions of learning.

- Government in gridlock over general opposition from leftist parties on liberalization steps taken by increasingly marginalized reformers, primarily Prime Minister Singh and Finance Minister Chidambaram.

Results: The current dominance of Indian offshore IT and BPO services fades. Due to the lack of growth opportunities, the IT industry loses its luster as a career option for new graduates, and they stop focusing on the IT and BPO industry, further reducing the availability of a qualified workforce.

Milestone Two

Budget 2008

Signposts:

- No significant budgetary allocations for education reform.

- No major allocations or financial incentives for infrastructure investments and infrastructure reform.

- Lack of FDI-friendly policies or discouragement of FDI through adverse policies.

Results: Enterprises globally are disenchanted by the lack of political will to drive real progress in improving the country's physical and other supporting infrastructure and look to other countries to address their needs. Equally disenchanted by lack of challenging career opportunities within the country, the brain drain of qualified Indian resources seeking better opportunities globally begins again.

Milestone Three

Central elections 2009

Signposts:

- Government formed from weak coalition of parties with divergent or conflicting agendas.

- Direct or indirect influence of Left on the government.

- Weak globalization credentials of prime minister.

Results: The continued integration of the Indian economy in general and the ICT industry in particular with the global economy is severely handicapped. India is increasingly marginalized on the global front.

Scenario Path Two: ICT Superpower (30 percent probability)

Milestone One

Government reforms progress by 2008

Signposts:

- Major pending policy decisions made and enforced; issues include FDI in retail, airport privatization, and labor reform.

- Major infrastructure projects (e.g., Golden Quadrilateral roads project, Mumbai Metro transport project, updated or new airports in Mumbai and elsewhere) completed or nearing completion.

- Metro Urban Renewal Project (MURP) achievements visible in at least 30 percent of targeted cities.

- Fundamental education reform initiated across the country, starting at primary level.

- Reformist voices in government, primarily Prime Minister Singh and Finance Minister Chidambaram, succeed in silencing the backward-looking Left.

- FDI flows into the country show strong growth (50 percent plus).

- Strong and growing venture capital activity in India.

- Growing equity markets increase capital inflows into the country.

Results: The dominance of Indian offshore IT and BPO services is reinforced and expands. There is an increase in the number of ICT start-ups in the country and significant IP generation, not just in services but in products as well. The ICT industry grows significantly as a percentage of GDP.

Milestone Two

Budget 2008

Signposts:

- Extensive budget allocations for education reform, including specific funding for curriculum reform and salary increases for teachers.

- Aggressive implementation of MURP tracked and reported on; extensive new allocations made.

- Tax incentives for infrastructure investments extended and strengthened.

- Budget allocation for power sector reform.

- ICT-friendly policies include continued rationalization and relaxation of taxation and custom duties across all segments of the ICT industry.

- Rupee made fully convertible.

Results: There is a surge in global enterprises' investments in India, through outsourcing relationships, captive centers, as well as increased R&D and IP generation activity. There are early signs of the education and training process starting to create a resource pool of "creative thinkers" as opposed to "order takers." Indian ICT companies expand their global presence at a faster rate, including an increase in acquisitions globally.

Milestone Three

Central elections 2009

Signposts:

- Single party majority gained by a reform-oriented government, ideally the current Congress Party–led government.

- No participation or presence in the government by the Left.

- Prime minister has clear and strong mandate for reforms and economic growth.

Results: India joins the ranks of the developed countries in terms of its global IT presence, not just as an offshore services destination, but also as an innovator and creator of valuable IP in the global IT industry. The IT industry, from both offshore and domestic perspectives, is a strong contributor to the GDP of the country and is successful in moving up the value chain to offer high-value IT resources, products, and services to the global community as well as to domestic industry.

Scenario Path Three: Digital Chasm (50 percent probability)

Milestone One

Government reforms progress by 2008

Signposts:

- Halting progress on major pending policy decisions and enforcement. These include FDI in retail, airport privatization, and labor reform.

- Major infrastructure projects like Golden Quadrilateral roads project, Mumbai Metro transport project, updated or new airports in Mumbai, New Delhi, Bangalore, Chennai, and Kolkata proceeding slowly but years behind schedule.

- MURP remains a paper plan; a few token projects completed.

- Pockets of education reform initiated, but no coordinated and aggressive national implementation; continuing debate on caste-based reservations in education.

- Reformist voices in government stalemated in many areas by retrograde voices of the Left.

- FDI flow into the country continues, though slowly.

Results: Indian offshore IT and BPO services maintain a static but increasingly commoditized presence on the global landscape. The larger Indian firms start to struggle to maintain their revenue and profitability amid the increased quantum of "low value" offshore services and resource quality constraints. The attempts of the Indian ICT industry to move up the value chain falter.

Milestone Two

Budget 2008

Signposts:

- Token allocations for education reform insufficient to produce meaningful, lasting results.

- No major allocation for infrastructure improvements.

- Weak or nonexistent allocations for power-sector reform.

- Minor allocations for MURP.

Results: Global enterprises view India as "just another option" for their outsourcing relationships and captive centers; India is no longer the dominant location. Other countries, notably China, gain increased mind-share and attention. Indian ICT companies start to shrink their global presence as reduced business growth makes an extensive global footprint unviable.

Milestone Three

Central elections 2009

Signposts:

- A reasonably aligned coalition comes into power but without adequate mandate to push through difficult reforms.

- No or minimal influence on the government by the Left.

- ICT-friendly government in general and prime minister specifically.

Results: The Indian IT industry maintains a steady but stagnant presence on the global landscape. However, India is increasingly seen as a destination suitable only for lower-value resource augmentation activities. It does not have a presence in high-capability, high-value work, except for a few companies' efforts. The IT industry is "just another option" for students pursuing a career and not the shining star it is today. The domestic industry actually benefits, as competition for the available IT resources is not as intense and they are able to attract and retain resources effectively.

Notes

Introduction

1. High-tech refers to the information technology, telecommunications, biotech, and nanotech industries.

2. Jason Dean, "GE Expects Sales in China to Double in Next 4 Years," *Wall Street Journal*, May 29, 2006, http://www.wsj.com.

3. Ibid.

4. Kathryn Kranhold, "GE to Try Another Push Into Indian Market," *Wall Street Journal*, May 30, 2006, http://www.wsj.com.

5. "GE Announces $250 Million Infrastructure Investment in India, Increase in Growth Targets," General Electric press release, May 30, 2006, http://www.ge.com.

6. "IBM Chairman and CEO Announces Plans to Triple Investment in India over Next Three Years," IBM press release, June 6, 2006, http://www.ibm.com.

7. Manjeet Kripalani and Peter Burrows, "Apple Follows Its Instincts out of India," *BusinessWeek*, June 5, 2006, http://www.businessweek.com/globalbiz/content/jun2006/gb20060605_273412.htm.

8. "U.S. Grills Microsoft, Google," The Hindu.com, February 17, 2006, http://www.hindu.com/2006/02/17/stories/2006021705281700.htm.

9. Peter Schwartz, *The Art of the Long View* (New York: Currency Doubleday, 1996).

10. Jeffrey Immelt, "What Makes a Company Great" (speech to the Economic Club of Washington, January 19, 2006), http://www.ge.com.

Chapter 1

1. Jasper Becker, *The Chinese* (London: John Murray, 2000), 110.

2. Jared Diamond, *Guns, Germs and Steel* (London: Chatto & Windus, 1997), 325–331.

3. Laurence J. Brahm, *Zhu Rongji & The Transformation of Modern China* (Singapore: John Wiley & Sons, 2002), 13.

4. Ibid., 130.

5. Ibid., 41.

6. Richard McGregor, "China's bad debts are 'under control,'" *Financial Times*, May 30, 2006, http://www.ft.com. Research reports noting concern about rising non-performing bank loans in China were issued in the first half of 2006 by UBS, Ernst & Young, McKinsey & Company, and PricewaterhouseCoopers.

7. Ibid.

8. Ng Aik Kwang, *Why Asians Are Less Creative than Westerners* (Singapore: Prentice Hall, 2001), 24.

9. World Bank, World Development Indicators Database, July 15, 2005, http://siteresources.worldbank.org/DATASTATISTICS/Resources/GNIPC.pdf.

10. Yougang Chen and Jacques Penhirin, "Marketing to China," in "China Today," *McKinsey Quarterly* (2004 special edition): 65, http://www.mckinseyquarterly.com/article_page.aspx?ar=1472.

11. Becker, *The Chinese*, 25.

12. Central Intelligence Agency, *The World Fact Book*, http://www.cia.gov/cia/publications/factbook/geos/ch.html.

13. Bloomberg News, "Tribunals to handle land rows," *The Standard*, July 4, 2006, http://www.thestandard.com.hk/news_detail.asp?pp_cat=5&art_id=22089&sid=8689503&con_type=1.

14. Chen and Penhirin, "Marketing to China," 73.

15. Dion Wiggins et al., "Internet shutdown: 200,000 China cybercafés shut in a day," E-17-1164, Gartner Research, June 25, 2002.

16. The US-China Business Council, "FDI in China (Total and US) 1979–2004," http://www.uschina.org/statistics/fdi_cumulative.html.

17. Ibid.

18. Lester R. Brown, "China Replacing the United States as World's Leading Consumer," Earth Policy Institute, February 16, 2005.

19. International Telecommunication Union, Mobile Cellular Subscribers, http://www.itu.int/ITU-D/ict/statistics/at_glance/cellular04.pdf.

20. Richard B. Freeman, "Does Globalization of the Scientific/Engineering Workforce Threaten US Economic Leadership?" working paper 11457, National Bureau of Economic Research.

21. Diana Farrell and Andrew J. Grant, "China's Looming Talent Shortage," *McKinsey Quarterly* no. 4 (2005): 70–79, http://www.mckinseyquarterly.com/article_page.aspx?ar=1685.

22. Freeman, "Does Globalization of the Scientific/Engineering Workforce Threaten US Economic Leadership?"

23. Farrell and Grant, "China's Looming Talent Shortage."

24. Joseph Hsu, e-mail interview with Jamie Popkin, April 25, 2006.

25. Ibid.

26. Farrell and Grant, "China's Looming Talent Shortage."

27. Ibid.

28. Jamie Popkin et al., "Hype Cycle for Emerging Technologies in China 2005," G00129035, Gartner Research, July 13, 2005.

Chapter 2

1. "Something New: Getting Serious about Innovation," *The Economist*, August 3, 2006, 38–39. The estimate is attributed to Professor Fang Xin of the Chinese Academy of Sciences.

2. Hao Xin and Gong Yidong, "Research Funding: China Bets Big on Big Science," *Science*, March 17, 2006, 1548–1549.

3. Ibid.

4. Associated Press, Beijing Bureau, "China's 15-year Technology Plan for Advances in Autos, Robots, Genetics," http://www.Financialexpress-bd.com.

5. Bob Hayward and Dion Wiggins, "Chinese Technology Companies Seek a Global Reach," G00123622, Gartner Research, September 14, 2004.

6. Richard P. Suttmeier, "Assessing China's Technology Potential," National Bureau of Asian Research, Science and Technology Department (Summer–Fall 2004): 457–491, http://www.nbr.org.publications/strategic_Asia/pdf/sa04_14sci-tech.pdf.

7. Jacqueline Heng, Minjoo Chon, and Tina T. Tang, "Market Overview: IT Services Providers in China, 2004," G00130604, Gartner Research, October 4, 2005.

8. Rolf Jester, Bob M. Hayward, and Dion Wiggins, "What Chinese IT Services Providers Must Do to Succeed in the Global Market," G00133637, Gartner Research, November 9, 2005.

9. Associated Press, "China's 15-year Technology Plan."

10. Vincent Fu, "Network and Internet Services and Service Providers in China, 2006," G00140976, Gartner Research, June 20, 2006.

11. Girish Trivedi, "Network and Internet Services and Service Providers in India, 2005," G00137257, Gartner Research, January 24, 2006.

12. Jitendra H. Jethanandani and Emma Rose, "Gartner Dataquest Market Databook, Asia/Pacific, October 2005," Gartner Research, December 12, 2005.

13. Jamie Popkin and Eng Chew, "State of the China Information and Communications Technology Industry—2005" (paper presented to Gartner Symposium ITXpo, Sydney, Australia, October 19, 2005).

14. Tina Tian, Ann Liang, Joy Yang, "China's Telecommunications Equipment Market Revenue Dropped 9.5 Percent in 1H05," G00131003, Gartner Research, October 3, 2005.

15. Jacqueline Heng, Minjoo Chon, and Tina T. Tang, "Market Overview: IT Services Providers in China, 2004," G00130604, Gartner Research, October 4, 2005.

16. Amy Teng et al., "Market Share: PCs, Asia/Pacific, 3Q05," G00135569, Gartner Research, November 8, 2005.

17. Jeanne Beyer, interview with Jamie Popkin, notes e-mailed April 28, 2006.

18. Joseph Hsu, interview with Jamie Popkin, notes e-mailed April 25, 2006.

19. Ibid.

20. Jeanne Beyer, interview with Jamie Popkin.

21. "Something New: Getting Serious about Innovation," 38–39.

22. Popkin and Chew, "State of the China Information and Communications Technology Industry—2005."

23. Vincent Fu, Ron Cowles, To Chee Eng, "Government Policies Limit Telecom Prospects in China Under WTO Agreement," G00129595, Gartner Research, August 9, 2005.

24. Ibid.

25. Oliver Xu, "China's Technology Standards Efforts Demand Wider Attention," G00129654, Gartner Research, September 21, 2005.

26. Bob Hayward and Dion Wiggins, "China's Domestic Standards Campaign Could Create Backlash," COM-22-0115, Gartner Research, April 28, 2004.

27. Ibid.

28. Dion Wiggins, "China, Intellectual Property Protection and the Big Picture," G00120976, Gartner Research, May 17, 2004.

29. Ibid.

30. Ibid.

31. Organisation for Economic Co-operation and Development, *OECD Fact Book,* 2005, http://caliban.sourceoecd.org/vl=2401453/cl=29/nw=1/rpsv/factbook/.

32. Subbiah Arunachalam, "Is Science in India on the Decline?" *Current Science* 83, no. 2 (2002): 108.

33. Diana Farrell and Andrew J. Grant, "China's Looming Talent Shortage," *McKinsey Quarterly* no. 4 (2005): 70–79.

34. Hao and Gong, "Research Funding: China Bets Big on Big Science."

35. David Barboza, "In a Computer Scientist's Fall, China Feels Robbed of Glory," *New York Times,* May 15, 2006, http://www.nytimes.com.

36. We are indebted in this analysis to several colleagues who analyze Asia's semiconductor markets. Related research includes: Klaus Rinnen, Bob Johnson, and Tom Yu, "China's Semiconductor Manufacturing Impact Will Be Muted," G00138029, Gartner Research, March 8, 2006; Jim Walker, Kay-Yang Tan, and Mark Stromberg, "China and Hong Kong Semiconductor Manufacturing Industry, 2Q06 Update," G00141422, Gartner Research, July 6, 2006. See also Kay-Yang Tan and James F. Hines, "Vendor Profile: Semiconductor Manufacturing International Corp.," G00140939, Gartner Research, August 1, 2006.

37. National Science Board, *Science and Engineering Indicators 2004* 1, NSB 04-1; 2, NSB 04-1A (Arlington, VA: National Science Foundation, 2004), 4–69.

Chapter 3

1. A fourth scenario is suggested by the lower-left quadrant in figure 3-1, labeled "World's (non-IT) Factory." None of the potential paths relevant to a discussion of the future landscape of China's ICT industry are included in this quadrant. As a result, the authors do not address the dynamics of this topic.

2. For comparison, figure 6-1, a similar two-by-two matrix graphic, with specific categories changed to reflect different dynamics in India's ICT landscape, is included in the chapter 6 analysis on India.

3. Tim Johnson, "China on the Rise," in "Moving Fast on the Tech Front," *Philadelphia Inquirer*, November 26, 2005.

4. http://www.caiwu.com.con/information/show.php?infoType=112@infoTID =0&infoID=3170; http://local.emagecompany.com/shanghai/guoyouqiye.htm.

5. Geoff Dyer, "GM and VW see surge in China sales," *Financial Times*, July 4, 2006, http://www.ft.com.

6. Sue Anne Tay and Mark Cabana, "Citigroup more equal than others," *Asia Times Online, China Business*, February 4, 2006, http://www.atimes.com.

7. Rick Carew, "Citigroup and Société Générale Battle for Rare Prize in China— Warts and All," *Wall Street Journal*, August 8, 2006, C1.

8. Richard McGregor, "Hu Makes IPR Pledge at Microsoft," *Financial Times*, April 19, 2006, http://www.ft.com.

9. Jason Dean and Rob Guth, "Microsoft Tries to Mimic Boeing's Fortunes in China," *Wall Street Journal*, April 17, 2006, A4.

10. Jim Yardley and Joseph Kahn, "Top Charge Dropped, but China Gives Times Researcher 3 Years," *New York Times*, August 25, 2006, A1.

11. "A Dark Signal from China," editorial, *New York Times*, May 21, 2006.

12. Charles Hutzler, "Expectations Are High for Beijing in 2008," Associated Press, February 22, 2006, http://www.Phillyburbs.com.

13. Ibid.

14. Xinhuanet News Service, "Beijing to build over 100 star hotels for 2008 Olympics," May 20, 2006.

15. Xinhuanet News Service, "Beijing to host 1st World Press Briefing for 2008 Games," May 18, 2006.

16. Beijing Olympic Committee for the 29th Olympic Games, "Olympiad Expected to Spur Economic Development," press release, May 18, 2006, http://www.en .Beijing2008.com.

17. Ibid.

18. Organisation for Economic Co-operation and Development, *OECD Fact Book*, 2005, http://caliban.sourceoecd.org/vl=2401453/cl=29/nw=1/rpsv/factbook/.

Chapter 4

1. *Times of India*, December 1, 2000.

2. Ministry of Finance, "Government of India, Economic Survey 2004–05," 111.

3. Partha Iyengar, "How to Assess Cities in India for Your IT Outsourcing Needs," G00126067, Gartner Research, March 11, 2005.

4. Census of India 2001, "Religious Community by Age Group and Sex," http://www.censusindia.net.

5. National Science Board, *Science and Engineering Indicators 2004* 1, NSB 04-1; 2, NSB 04-1A (Arlington, VA: National Science Foundation, 2004), 2–34.

6. Ibid., 11.

7. Department of Education, Government of India, "Education Statistics," http://www.education.nic.in/htmlweb/edusta.htm.

8. "The Emerging Global Labor Market, Part II," McKinsey & Company, June 2005, 23.

9. Subbiah Arunachalam, "Is Science in India on the Decline?" *Current Science* 83, no. 2 (2002): 108.

10. Human Rights Watch, "We Have No Orders to Save You," HRW Index No. C1403, April 30, 2002, http://www.hrw.org.

11. On the importance of understanding diversity, it is worth noting that one of the causes of a major 1857 Indian revolt against British ambitions was an uprising by Hindu and Muslim soldiers in the British army, responding to rumors that their guns were greased by cow or pig fat. This was deeply religiously offensive to Hindus and Muslims, respectively.

12. Pratap Bhanu Mehta, "The Nationalist Movement," in *Understanding Contemporary India*, ed. Sumit Ganguly and Neil DeVotta (London: Lynne Rienner, 2003), 60.

13. The Congress Party controlled India's government from 1947 to 1977, 1980 to 1989, and for shorter periods since then.

14. World Bank, "Doing Business," http://www.doingbusiness.org/ExploreEconomies/Default.aspx?economyid=19.

15. A good source for data on the great array of elections within India can be found at www.indian-elections.com.

16. A good account of the Karnataka Election Watch research can be found in "Could These Candidates Be Lawmakers," *India Together*, May 2004, http://www.indiatogether.org/2004/may/gov-karpolls.htm.

17. Partha Iyengar and Jamie Popkin, "The State of the Indian ICT Industry, 2005" (paper presented to Gartner Summit India, Mumbai, July 2005).

18. Reserve Bank of India, "Foreign Investment Inflows, 1990–91 to 2004–05," http://rbidocs.rbi.org.in/rdocs/Publications/DOCs/66017.xls.

19. Reserve Bank of India, "Report on Currency and Finance 2003–04," http://rbidocs.rbi.org.in/rdocs/PublicationReport/Pdfs/59580.pdf.

20. World Health Organization, "Selected Indicators Related to Reproductive, Maternal and Newborn Health," http://www.who.int/whr/2005/annex/annex8.xls.

21. Barbara Crossette, "The Role of Women," in *Understanding Contemporary India*, 139.

22. Nandan Nilekani, "Bangalored in Beijing," *Indian Express*, June 5, 2005.

23. Amy Waldman, "Mile by Mile, India Paves a Smoother Road to Its Future," *New York Times*, December 4, 2005.

24. Ian Marriott, "Consider Offshore Options Around the Globe," G00128032, Gartner Research, June 14, 2005.

25. Iyengar and Popkin, "The State of the Indian ICT Industry, 2005."

Chapter 5

1. Partha Iyengar and Jamie Popkin, "The State of the Indian ICT Industry, 2005" (paper presented to Gartner Summit India, Mumbai, July 2005).

2. Robert De Souza, Michele Caminos, and Twiggy Lo, "Forecast: IT Outsourcing, Asia/Pacific, 2003–2009," G00130470, Gartner Research, August 17, 2005.

3. Jitendra Jethanandani and Emma Rose, "Gartner Dataquest Market Databook Asia/Pacific October 2005," G00136901, Gartner Research, December 12, 2005; George Shiffler et al., *Gartner Dataquest Market Databook,* September 2005; Update, October 27, 2005.

4. National Science Board, *Science and Engineering Indicators 2004* 1, NSB 04-1; 2, NSB 04-1A (Arlington, VA: National Science Foundation, 2004), 3–34.

5. Sujay Chohan, former Gartner colleague, interview by Bob Hayward for Jamie Popkin, Mumbai, September 2006, to formulate views on the development of the Indian IT industry.

6. Rolf Jester, "Market Trends: IT Services, India, 2004–2009," G00130072, Gartner Research, August 19, 2005.

7. Ibid.

8. Bhawani Shankar, Kobita Desai, and Sumit Malik, "Telecommunications Network Outsourcing Has Promise and Risk," G00122380, Gartner Research, September 7, 2004.

9. Saritha Rai, "World Business Briefing/Asia: Bharti Posts Profit Rise," *New York Times,* July 27, 2006, http://www.nytimes.com.

10. We are grateful to colleagues Kobita Desai, Robin Simpson, Andy Kok Mun Woo, and Nick Ingelbrecht for this analysis. Their extensive user survey and detailed conclusions were published by Gartner early in 2006. For more information, see Kobita Desai, Robin Simpson, Andy Kok Mun Woo, and Nick Ingelbrecht, "User Survey: Businesses' Plans for Mobile Technology, India, 2005," G00137073, Gartner Research, February 2, 2006.

11. Shankar, Desai, and Malik, "Telecommunications Network Outsourcing Has Promise and Risk."

12. Ian Marriott, "Consider Offshore Options around the Globe," G00128032, Gartner Research, June 14, 2005.

13. Partha Iyengar et al., "Hype Cycle for Emerging Technologies in India, 2005," G00128138, Gartner Research, May 26, 2005.

14. Partha Iyengar, "How to Assess Cities in India for Your IT Outsourcing Needs," G00126067, Gartner Research, March 11, 2005.

15. International Telecommunication Union, World Telecommunication Development Report 2003, http://www.itu.int/ITU-D/ict/statistics/.

16. Iyengar et al., "Hype Cycle for Emerging Technologies in India, 2005."

17. International Telecommunication Union, World Telecommunication Development Report 2003, http://www.itu.int/ITU-D/ict/statistics/.

18. Jennifer Wu et al., "Forecast: PCs, Asia/Pacific, 2003–2009," G00126658, Gartner Research, March 11, 2005.

19. Sujay Chohan and Ian Marriott, "India Dominates in Offshore BPO, but Will Face Challenges," G00129014, Gartner Research, June 24, 2005.

20. Azim Premji (speech to announce the winning schools of the Azim Premji Foundation Learning Guarantee Programme, Bangalore, India, February 14, 2004).

21. See "Intel plans $500-mn spend in India," *India Daily*, December 3, 2005.

22. Partha Iyengar, "India-Based IT Service Providers Tap Into China's Potential," G00123416, Gartner Research, March 1, 2005.

23. Ministry of Finance, Government of India, "Economic Survey 2004–05" (budget presented to Parliament of India, February 25, 2005), 112, http://indiabudget .nic.in/es2004-05/esmain.htm.

24. Rebecca S. Scholl, "Business Process Outsourcing at the Crossroads," ITES-WW-MT-0103, Gartner Research, January 31, 2002.

Chapter 6

1. Ian Marriott, "Offshore Services—2006 and Beyond: Choices, Challenges and Change," (paper presented at Gartner Outsourcing Summit 2006, Tokyo, April 2006).

2. India Infoline News, "Intel Centrino . . . dual mobile technology unveiled," January 10, 2006.

3. "Intel to Make India Its Global Hub," *Times of India*, May 21, 2006.

4. John Ribeiro, "Symantec India to Identify Products for Global Markets," IDG News Service, September 21, 2005.

5. Ibid. Symantec is developing product ideas with Wipro for customers using enterprise business software from SAP of Walldorf, Germany. The Symantec center also is pursuing the disaster recovery (DR) market, concluding that some customers in India match the sophistication of DR customers anywhere in the world.

6. Siddharth Srivastava, "India Animated by Special Effects Outsourcing," *Asia-TimesOnline*, April 21, 2005, http://www.atimes.com/atimes/South_Asia/GD21Df05 .html.

7. Noshir F. Kaka, "Running a Customer Service Center in India: An Interview with the Head of Operations for Dell India," *McKinsey Quarterly*, Web exclusive, May 2006, http://www.mckinseyquarterly.com.

8. World Economic Forum, "Global Competition Report, 2004–2005," www.we-forum.org.

9. Erica J. Bever, Elizabeth Stephenson, and David W. Tanner, "How India's Executives See the World," in "Fulfilling India's Promise," *McKinsey Quarterly* (2005 special edition): 34–41.

10. Room rates during Bangalore's busiest months between October and March were between $250 and $300 per night in 2005, equal to rates in New York or San Francisco. See Moumita Bakshi Chatterjee and Bharat Kumar, "Can't Rent Them?

Own Them! IT Companies See Value in In-house Accommodations for Clients," *Hindu Business Line*, December 26, 2005.

11. Ibid.

12. Parvathi Menon, "Politics of Infrastructure," *Frontline*, November 5–18, 2005, http://www.flonnet.com/fl2223/stories/20051118003204300.htm. Government-industry relations in Bangalore reached a low point in October 2005, with Congress Party officials and industry leaders, including Infosys's N. R. Narayana Murthy, trading charges as IT executives from one hundred fifty Indian companies and one hundred twenty foreign companies gathered for an important annual IT conference in Bangalore. The Congress Party had lost ground in the state of Karnataka, which includes Bangalore, in the 2004 elections, a period when the agriculture sector was in hard times. A year later, Congress Party officials publicly were keeping their distance from IT business leaders. "We cannot have islands of prosperity in an ocean of poverty," said a leading Congress Party official in the Karnataka government.

13. Reuters, "Communism and Computers Mix Well in Calcutta," May 21, 2004.

14. "The Thin Red Line: A Bastion of Indian Communism Rebrands Itself," *The Economist*, May 6, 2006.

15. Musharrat Habib, "Indian Communist Party Chief Minister of West Bengal State Provides First Signal of Embracing Outsourcing—Chinese Model Ideal for Indian Communists," *The India Daily*, September 25, 2005, http://www.indiadaily.com /editorial/4723.asp.

16. Partha Iyengar, "How to Assess Cities in India for Your IT Outsourcing Needs," G00126067, Gartner Research, March 11, 2005.

17. Paranjoy Guha Thakurta, "High Salaries Can Reverse Brain Drain," Inter-Press Service, May 9, 2006. The article quoted the deputy dean of the Indian School of Business, Agit Rangnekar, on hints of a counterattack by Indian companies in salary bids. "What was especially surprising was the fact that the highest salary in U.S. dollars was offered by an Indian technology company with international operations," he said. "It is significant that Indian companies are today willing to pay global salaries to talented young graduates so as to be able to compete effectively in the world market—that's the big message."

18. Anand Mahindra, "What Will It Take for India to Become the No. 1 FDI Destination in the World?" *Business Today*, January 15, 2006.

19. Robyn Meredith, "Split Personality: To Exploit Explosive New Growth in Asia, Consumer Electronics Giant Philips Uses Very Different Business Plans for China and India," *Forbes*, October 17, 2005.

20. H. Sykes, "Will Booming Bangalore's Bubble Burst?" BBC News, January 4, 2006.

21. Speaking at a fifty-year anniversary dinner for IIT alumni in Silicon Valley in 2003, Bill Gates said that in the prior two years Microsoft had hired more than fifty IIT graduates "and we're doing our best to increase that number." (Remarks by Bill Gates, India Institute of Technology Fiftieth Anniversary Celebration Dinner, Cupertino, CA, January 17, 2003), Microsoft.com, http://www.microsoft.com/billgates/speeches/2003 /01-17iit.asp.

22. Kathryn Kranhold, "GE to Try Another Push Into Indian Market," *Wall Street Journal,* May 30, 2006, http://www.wsj.com.

23. Ibid. The article also said GE's vice chairman, David Calhoun, believed that the Indian government was more eager to invest in airports, hospitals, railroads, and power systems, including nuclear power.

Chapter 7

1. "India and China Agree to Study Regional Trade Agreement," Thehindu.com, March 17, 2006.

2. Chetan Ahya et al., "India and China: New Tigers of Asia, Part II," Morgan Stanley Research, June 2006.

3. "A Tale of Two Countries," Indian Brand Equity Foundation, http://www.ibef.org/artdispview.aspx?art_id=3151&cat_id=390&page=1

4. *IMD World Competitiveness Yearbook,* 2006, 7.

5. Richard Milne, "German Blue Chips Fear Eastern Rivals," *Financial Times,* August 28, 2006, http://www.ft.com.

6. Ibid.

7. "Too Early to Tell: A Much-Vaunted Sino-Indian 'Strategic Partnership' Is Only in Its Infancy," *The Economist,* April 14, 2005.

8. Pallavi Aiyar, "Neighbours Building an IT Highway," *The Hindu,* March 11, 2006.

9. "TCS Signs Shareholder Promoters Agreement to Establish Software Joint Venture with Chinese Firms," Tata Consultancy Services, press release, July 24, 2006.

10. Aiyar, "Neighbours Building an IT Highway."

11. Giuseppe De Filippo, Jun Hou, and Christopher Ip, "Can China Compete in IT Services?" *McKinsey Quarterly,* no. 1 (2005): 10–11.

12. "TCS Signs Shareholder Promoters Agreement."

13. "TCS to Hire 30,000 Engineering Grads," *India Times Infotech,* August 21, 2006, http://www.infotech.indiatimes.com.

14. Bloomberg News, "Infy Plumps for China," April 17, 2006, http://www.Financialexpress.com.

15. "China's Neusoft to Set Up Software Firm in B'lore," *Economic Times,* August 1, 2006, http://www.infotech.indiatimes.com.

16. Thomas L. Friedman, *The World Is Flat: A Brief History of the Twenty-First Century* (New York: Farrar, Straus and Giroux, 2005), 425–429.

17. Ibid.

18. Khozem Merchant, "IBM to Invest $6bn in India Over Three Years," *Financial Times,* June 6, 2006, http://www.ft.com.

19. Kathryn Kranhold, "GE to Try Another Push Into Indian Market," *Wall Street Journal,* May 30, 2006, wsj.com; Jason Dean, "GE Expects Sales in China to Double in Next 4 Years," *Wall Street Journal,* May 29, 2006, http://www.wsj.com.

20. Kranhold, "GE to Try Another Push Into Indian Market."

21. Associated Press, "Motorola to Invest $100M in India Plant," *New York Times*, June 7, 2006, http://www.nytimes.com.

22. Kobita Desai, Gartner Inc. analysis, e-mailed to authors, May 1, 2006.

23. Paivi Munter, "Nokia in Reach of 40% Market Share," *Financial Times*, April 20, 2006, http://www.ft.com.

24. "China Decries India's Attitude-Axe!" March 16, 2006, http://www.Financial-express.com.

25. Ibid.

Chapter 8

1. "India-China Friendship Year Begins," *Times of India Online*, January 2, 2006.

2. "India, China to Launch Activities, Marking Friendship Year," January 24, 2006, http://www.Chinaview.cn.

3. "Bharat Forge Ties Up with FAW Corp to Enter China," *Hindu Business Line*, December 8, 2005.

4. "Opening Ceremony of FAW Bharat Forge (Changchun) Co., Ltd.," Bharat Forge press release, March 20, 2006, http://www.Bharatforge.com.

5. Ibid.

6. Ibid.

7. The open-sky policy in India is officially opposed by the Communist Party of India (Marxist), which argues that increased competition could cause a loss of revenues and jobs at India's largest airlines, Air India and Indian Airlines. See "CITU Opposes Open-Sky policy," *People's Organ*, January 9, 2005, http://pd.cpim.org/2005/0109/01092005_citu.htm.

8. "Beijing Wants India Inc. to Pick Up Stake in Chinese PSUs," April 20, 2006, http://www.Financialexpress.com.

9. Ibid.

10. "Chinese Steel Companies Exploring Opportunities in India," *Hindu Business Line*, April 18, 2006.

Chapter 9

1. We are indebted to Gartner colleague Kristian Steenstrup for this case analysis. Steenstrup, based in Australia, is an expert on technologies in the global energy and utilities industries. See "Mincom and Neusoft Gain Enterprise Asset Management Credibility in China Through Partnership," G00129113, Gartner Research, June 29, 2005.

2. C. K. Prahalad, *The Fortune at the Bottom of the Pyramid: Eradicating Poverty through Profits* (Upper Saddle River, NJ: Wharton School Publishing, 2004).

3. Ibid.

4. Khozem Merchant, "Final Frontier for the Shampoo Sellers," *Financial Times*, May 20, 2003, http://www.ft.com.

5. William E. Hoover Jr., "Making China Your Second Home Market: An Interview with the CEO of Danfoss," *McKinsey Quarterly*, no. 1 (2006): 84–93.

6. "Nokia Wins $125M Bharti Deal," Nokia press release, August 23, 2005, http://www.Unstrung.com.

7. Ibid.

8. Jeffrey Immelt, chairman and CEO of GE, in a speech at Cornell University, April 15, 2004. He said that twenty-five airports were under construction in China at the time, compared with one new airport built in the United States in the previous twenty-five years. See "The Innovation Imperative," http://www.ge.com/files/usa/company/news/cornell_transcript.pdf.

9. Our Hong-Kong based Gartner colleague Dion Wiggins and former colleague Bob M. Hayward developed this analysis for their paper, "Foreign Companies Face Unique Challenges in China," COM-21-9510, Gartner Research, April 26, 2004.

10. Jeffrey Immelt, "What Makes a Great Company" (speech to the Economic Club of Washington, January 19, 2006), http://www.ge.com.

11. We again are grateful to our colleague Kristian Steenstrup for this analysis. The ideas were first presented in his research note, "Choosing Between Integrated or Autonomous ERP in China," COM-22-5074, Gartner Research, May 4, 2004.

12. Azim Premji's comment was in answer to a question on Wipro's quarterly earnings conference call with investment analysts, January 18, 2006. Wipro's chief financial officer, Suresh Senapaty, added that Wipro's staff in Shanghai Pudong will be a "much higher number" within a year or two. For transcript of telephone conference statements, questions and answers, see http://www.wipro.com/investors/pdf_files/Transcript-wipro-Jan-2006-1:30pm.pdf.

13. Nitza Hidalgo, "Multicultural Teacher Introspection," in *Freedom's Plow: Teaching in the Multicultural Classroom*, ed. T. Perry and J. Fraser (New York: Routledge/Taylor & Francis Group, LLC, 1993). © 1993.

14. Richard E. Nisbett, *The Geography of Thought: How Asians and Westerners Think Differently . . . and Why* (New York: Free Press, 2003), 25–26. Excerpted and adapted with permission. © 2003 by Richard Nisbett.

15. Ibid.

16. Ibid., 44.

17. Kirpal Singh, interview with Partha Iyengar, Chongquing, China, May 10, 2006.

Index

About the Authors

James (Jamie) M. Popkin is a group vice president and research fellow emeritus in Gartner Research responsible for the Business Intelligence and Information Management research group. Prior to this position, Jamie was responsible for Gartner research content strategy in China, India, and Korea; served as worldwide Head of Research for Vertical Industries and Gartner Asia/Pacific and Japan; and was Chairman of Gartner U.S. and Japan Symposia/ITxpo. Jamie currently serves as a senior adviser to the China Business Continuity Management Association. He has extensive experience in public speaking in Asia, including the Seoul Digital Forum; the Sino-India IT Industry Conference, sponsored by the Beijing National Development and Reform Council; Waseda University Business School Marketing Forum; Info China 2004–2005, sponsored by CCID and the China State Council; and the Korea Ministry of Information and Communication Annual Conference. Jamie has also served as a board member of the Association for Image and Information Management (AIIM) International Board of Directors. Jamie earned a BA in Economics from Connecticut College and a Master of Public Policy from the John F. Kennedy School of Government at Harvard University.

Partha Iyengar is a vice president and research director in Gartner Research. In his current role, he is responsible for research coverage in global software development, global sourcing, and tracking IT industry developments for India and China. Prior to returning to Pune, India, in 1995 to establish Gartner's operations there, Partha was based in Gartner's global headquarters in Stamford, Connecticut, and was Head of Applications Development in its internal IT organization.

A frequent speaker at various national and international forums, Partha is regularly quoted in international media and publications as an expert on various issues related to the dynamics of globalization and its impact on the various countries affected by it.

Partha earned his BE (Mechanical) degree at the College of Engineering, Pune, India; his MS (Mechanical) degree at the New Jersey Institute of Technology in Newark, New Jersey; and his MBA from Rensselaer Polytechnic Institute in Troy, New York.